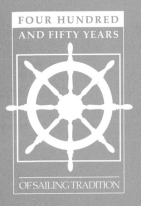

FOUR HUNDRED
AND FIFTY YEARS

OF SAILING TRADITION

Bob Covarrubias

First edition
Edited by Craig Arnold and Sandra Roberts
Illustrations by Jim DeWitt
Book Design by Bette McHenry

Library of Congress Catalog Card Number
91-65913
Sullaway, Neva 1952-
Sailing in San Diego – A Pictorial History
ISBN1-879589-00-1
Printed in the United States of America

Published by TCS Publishing, Inc.
10525 Vista Sorrento Parkway, Suite 101
San Diego, CA 92121-2746

Dedicated

To San Diego's City Founders...
Explorers
Adventurers
Speculators
Innovators
City Builders
To the Sailors, One and All

Foreward

The following pages describe, in a very pleasing manner, the history of sailing and its long-range importance for San Diego. Beginning with the square-rigged ships that brought supplies of all descriptions (including coal from Newcastle), to the advent of recreational sailing, San Diego has a long and interesting history under sail.

Having lived on Coronado Island during its very early days of development, it was of special interest to me to watch the great sailing ships docking and unloading lumber from the Pacific Northwest for the building of the famous Hotel del Coronado, as well as other buildings.

Another interesting aspect of life in those days was that fishing for the local markets was done by sailing boats of all descriptions, including Chinese junks, which were common before the introduction of the marine engine.

Before the days of yachting as we know it, the fishing boats were rented on Saturdays and Sundays to those who loved to sail; the Portuguese and Italian fishermen were very religious and did not fish on those days.

Yachting has played an important role in the development of the San Diego area. John D. Spreckels, who became a leading developer of San Diego and Coronado, first came here on his sailing yacht *Lurline*.

Spreckels had sailed *Lurline* down from San Francisco, and immediately saw the opportunities in this beautiful area.

In 1904, Sir Thomas Lipton presented the San Diego Yacht Club with a beautiful trophy, which is still important today among the racing fleets. In 1913, Lipton visited San Diego, which further brought attention to sailing yachts.

In 1908, the yacht *Lady Maude* was the first to sail in the Honolulu Race, representing the San Diego Yacht Club, which again drew attention to the use of sail for recreation.

My family has played an important role in the history of yachting in San Diego. Alonzo, my brother, was the founding father of the San Diego Yacht Club, and five members of my family have been Commodores over the years. Many famous names could be added as being important in the history of sailing in San Diego. Captain Lew B. Harris, Clem Stose and Ash Bown are just a few names that come to mind.

The new San Diego Convention Center has featured the use of sails in its design, alluding to the importance of sailing since San Diego's discovery.

The author of this book has described the beauty, the pleasures, the fame and fortunes created by the use of sail. And so we must thank Aeolus, the god of wind, for providing the power that made all this possible.

Joseph E. Jessop Sr.
July, 1991

Acknowledgements

Though many people envision the author's task as being a solitary one, it requires the help of almost everyone related to the subject at hand! I would like to thank Joseph Jessop Sr. for lending me his vision, which has viewed nearly a century of San Diego history. Without his very special insight, I might have lost the essence of the story altogether.

The San Diego Historical Society, San Diego Maritime Museum and the San Diego Yacht Club provided a direct link to the past by supplying the research materials and photographs necessary to enliven the vision. I cannot stress enough my heartfelt thanks to the San Diego Historical Society (with Jane and Larry Booth at the helm), and the fleet of research assistants and volunteers who offered endless hours of assistance. The San Diego Maritime Museum houses a remarkable selection of nautical history and photographs. A great debt of gratitude goes to Craig Arnold (S.D.M.M.'s librarian and editor of *Mains'l Haul)*, whose editing skills and grasp of maritime history saved me from some embarrassing blunders.

The San Diego Yacht Club, headed by outgoing Commodore Frank Radford and incoming Commodore Sandy Purdon, made every effort to make the resources of the Club available to me, even to the extent of allowing me to unscrew photos from their walls! Many members of the Club, most prominently Jack Sutphen and Tom Wilson, generously gave of their time in reviewing parts of the text. I would especially like to thank Charles La Dow for his very comprehensive history of the San Diego Yacht Club, *The Ships, The House, And The Men*. Without Mr. La Dow's proclivity for detail, the history of yachting in San Diego would be much more obscure.

Each yacht club, in their turn, supplied their own histories. The Mission Bay Yacht Club's history has been very carefully preserved, and it is to the credit of Eleanor and "Mac" McLaughlin to have so meticulously organized that history. When a club was newly re-established, as was the Chula Vista Yacht Club, manager Carol Whipple kindly headed me in the proper direction for further information.

This book was designed to be a pictorial history, and so I must thank those photographers, both named and unnamed, for their extraordinary talent. Where early historical photos (late 1800's) appear to have some imperfections, they will hopefully be appreciated for their historical perspective. I am very grateful to the Rosenfeld Collection staff, including Collection Manager Elizabeth Parker Rafferty, assistant Deborah DiGregorio and researcher Jack MacFadyen – not only for making their extraordinary collection available to me but for their efficiency in handling my selection from over a million photographic images. While researching the history of the America's Cup, I had the very great pleasure of meeting Philip Crowther Jr. (Museum of Yachting, Newport, Rhode Island) who has painstakingly recorded the history of the Cup via a voluminous newspaper collection dating to the 1800's. San Francisco artist Jim DeWitt contributed his unique talent to the book, enhancing our impressions with lively strokes of color and exciting images.

I would also like to thank prominent San Diego families, along with the Jessops, who very generously shared their own personal histories and photographs with me: the Kettenburgs, Fetters and Islers, Burnhams, Frosts, Driscolls, Reynolds and Thomases...this list alone could go on for several pages!

In terms of unearthing information, I am indebted to my number one researcher Roger Lakner, who spent untold hours searching for those elusive details which round out a condensed history.

Also included in the long list of acknowledgments are:

Dale Frost and the Port of San Diego, Steve Christman and the Nautical Heritage Society, the Orange County Marine Institute, John Willet and Frank Roseman of the Tall Ship Society, Jackie Dooley of the UCSD Library, Special Collections; Carolyn Rainey of Scripps Institution of Oceanography Archives, UCSD; Captain Rich Goben of Invader Cruises, Gary Wiseman of North Sails, Scott Tempesta of Sobstad Sailmakers, C.F. Koehler of Koehler Kraft, Greg Stewart of Nelson/Marek Yacht Design, and Filmbase, which worked small miracles on many of the historical black and white photographs.

Special thanks to the whole team at TCS Publishing who helped realize this book.

Finally, I would like to thank my husband Stephen, for his endless support and enthusiasm throughout each phase of the project, and for his ability to keep our ship steady as she goes....

Thank You.

FOUR HUNDRED
AND FIFTY YEARS

OF SAILING TRADITION

Table of Contents

Introduction

Exactly how *Sailing in San Diego - A Pictorial History* came about might be worth a few words. The idea was initially conceived along San Diego Bay's foreshore. There is a clearing abaft the stern of the *Star of India*, before you arrive at the walkway, that takes you onto the *Berkeley*, where quite a breathtaking view of the harbor can be secured. My friend and maritime historian Captain Ray Ashley and I paused for a moment to take in the shimmering late afternoon panorama. Ray is a native San Diegan and has skippered various boats on San Diego Bay for more than a decade, and I had served as his crew for a few of those years.

Ray knew just about every square inch of San Diego's waterspace. He also harbored a fair bit of knowledge about San Diego's history, and asked if I'd like to have a look at San Diego's first racing yacht – a fishing boat called *Butcher Boy*. At the time, *Butcher Boy* was housed at the B Street Pier, which was just a short walk from where we stood. When I saw the sturdy little vessel lying up on the hard, I knew that she was not so much disregarded as waiting her turn to represent that portion of history which was nearly lost.

Butcher Boy somehow became my link with San Diego's sailing history. She dated back to 1902, and I could touch her planks and feel ninety years of history at my finger tips. Research had begun.

It was a daunting enterprise to undertake a book on the history of sailing in San Diego. First, it required the consideration: Where should such a history begin? If that wasn't troublesome enough, one must consider the debate: What does "sailing" encompass? I piled up the history books, sailing manuals and dictionaries in a desperate attempt to find guidelines. The more deeply immersed I became, the hazier the boundaries. Finally, in an effort to get the project under way, I shoved the pile of books aside, and decided that the history should begin with San Diego's discovery!

"Sailing," true to its dictionary term, encompasses "the sport of managing a sailboat, as for racing." In the early historical context, I thought I might broaden the meaning to include "sailing ships – as driven by wind on sails." All was well, then, until I threw in the word "yacht" and had to begin the search all over again. The Dutch supplied us with this word, with its early derivation from "^jaghtschip,' or a pursuit ship (i.e. against pirates), any of the various relatively small ships for pleasure cruises, racing, etc." At last I had a launching point.

Having an inadequate knowledge of naval vessels, fishing boats and cargo ships, I thought it best to stay within my realm of understanding. My emphasis on sailing was in no way meant to lessen the importance of other maritime presences in San Diego. With those considerations swept under the rug, I could get on with the matter at hand: How does one compress 450 years of sailing into one book, which at some point in its life might require lifting off the coffee table? Well, why not hold firmly to the old adage and let the photos tell the story!

We embark, then, upon a rich history, which abounds in adventure, courage, discovery, harshness and beauty, all of which began with two Spanish ships rounding the Point Loma headland in 1542. We will chart the voyager's course through 450 years to a climactic moment in our sailing history – the year 1992, when the America's Cup XXVIII will be raced in San Diego, California. Then, on to the new horizon beyond....

Juan Cabrillo sailed from Puerto de Navidad, New Spain in 1542 (this port was located near Manzanillo, Mexico).

Cabrillo's galleon San Salvador has been described as being 85' to 90' long with a crew of sixty to one hundred men. As one might imagine, the conditions were, at best, primitive. With no bunks below, the crew slept on deck. The area below deck was reserved for cargo, which often included animals such as horses. It was not surprising, under the circumstances, that crews suffered not only severe hardships, but death from scurvy and dysentery.

Chapter One

El Puerto de San Miguel

1542

◆

Historians have credited the Portuguese navigator João Rodrigues Cabrilho as being the first European to sail into San Diego Bay. If Juan Cabrillo (Spanish spelling) had truly been recognized as the official founder of San Diego, the 1992 America's Cup would be sailed in San Miguel Bay!

Sailing under the Spanish flag, Cabrillo commanded two ships *San Salvador* and *Victoria*. A summary of Cabrillo's journal describes his landfall and subsequent entry into the bay on September 28, 1542:

"On the following Thursday they went about six leagues [approximately 18 nautical miles] along a coast running north-northwest, and discovered a port, closed and very good, which they named San Miguel. It is in thirty-four and one third degrees. Having cast anchor in it, they went ashore where there were people. Three of them waited, but all the rest fled. To these three they gave some presents and they said by signs that in the interior men like the Spaniards had passed. They gave signs of great fear. On the night of this day they went ashore from the ship to fish with a net, and it appears that here there were some Indians, and they began to shoot them with arrows and wounded three men."

Cabrillo noted in his log a latitude of 34° 20' North Latitude, instead of its correct latitude of 32° 40'. Though his calculations were off by 2 degrees and 20' (or 140 sea miles), one might consider the crude charts and instruments he had to work with.

It is to Cabrillo's credit that he came within a few degrees of the correct position. It was no small feat to sail two ships where none had passed before.

Among the instruments used were terrestrial globes, wooden and bronze compasses, magnetic needles, hourglasses and a wooden log to be towed astern. These navigational instruments were vital in establishing a latitude; however, they didn't provide the information needed to determine a correct longitude. (Both latitude and longitude are needed to establish a precise position.) The calculations for longitude are based on the circumference of the earth. In Cabrillo's time, this measurement was based on an unreliable reference, which dated back to the Second Century B.C.

As Juan Cabrillo sailed out of the bay on October 3 (after a stay of only six days), he named the bay "San Miguel," in honor of St. Michael the Archangel.

The statue celebrating Juan Cabrillo and his arrival in San Diego can be seen atop Point Loma. It is one of the many sights and attractions of Cabrillo National Monument.

Neva Sullaway

1602

◆

The bay rested quietly for another sixty years. No ship graced her waters until 1602, when Sebastián Vizcaíno sailed under orders from Spain, to explore from Cape San Lucas to Cape Mendocino. He was to chart the coastline, noting the entrances to ports, as he made his way northward. He was not to change the names of any of the landmarks already mapped by Cabrillo.

Under his command were four small ships: the *San Diego*, *San Tomas*, *Tres Reyes* and a smaller unnamed boat. In an apparent attempt to leave his own mark on history, Vizcaíno renamed every landmark previously charted, in sharp defiance of his orders.

Among the passengers on board the *San Diego*, was Fr. Antonio de la Ascensión, a Carmelite friar, who assiduously kept a journal of the passage from New Spain (Mexico). Fr. Ascensión described their entrance into the Port of San Miguel (soon to be renamed San Diego) on November 10, 1602:

"The country surrounding the port was very fertile and near the beach there are very fine meadows. The general and Father Antonio [another friar on board] with other soldiers made a turn around all the ensenada [inlet] and looked over the country. They were pleased to see its fertility and good character, but what gives them the greatest pleasure was the extensiveness, capacity and security of the port, its good depth and many fish."

Father Ascensión proved to be an astute observer. He also noted sparkling golden pyrites in the sand along the foreshore, "a sure sign that there must be gold mines in the mountains."

After Vizcaíno's expedition, there would not be another ship entering the bay for 167 years. It appears that the constant buffeting from the nor'westers proved to be a great setback for the sailing ships, which struggled to make headway against them. Even the lure of vast treasures such as gold, silver and pearls, or the search for the mythical Straits of Anian (as a northern trade route to the Far East) would not draw Spain's attention back to the Californias.

1769

◆

Rumors began to circulate regarding the presence of Russian and English ships along Spain's Alta California coastline. The time had come for Spain to re-establish its hold on California.

Three Spanish ships, representing the sea expedition of 1769, set out from La Paz, while two land parties, which had originally set off on foot from Loreto, regrouped at Velicáta (near the present sight of El Rosario). Their orders were to establish a military foothold in San Diego, while the missionaries would help colonize the settlements. In most cases, the "colonizing" referred to bringing the Christian faith to the Indians.

➤

The original site for the mission and military outpost was located in the Presidio near Old Town. Today, the Junipero Serra Museum rests on the knoll overlooking the former site of the Presidio.

Stephen Simpson

This map depicts the land and sea expedition of 1769. Three ships left from Lá Paz, and the land expedition with Portolá and Fr. Serra departed from Velicáta.

The accounts of both the sea and land journeys are a testimonial to a land hard won. The overland trek was led by Don Gaspar de Portolá, with Fr. Junipero Serra stoically setting out with an infected leg. Much has been written about Fr. Serra, and it is a great tribute to his unflinching faith and bravery that he endured the journey, and went on to establish the first of California's twenty-one missions – Mission San Diego de Alcala.

While those on the overland expedition struggled over the harsh, barren wilderness of cacti and mesquite, a more perilous journey awaited those who had set sail from La Paz.

The smallest of the three ships, the *San Jose,* cleared Cape San Lucas and was never seen again. After a grueling 57-day voyage, the *San Antonio* arrived in San Diego Bay with more than half the crew incapacitated from scurvy and dysentery. It would take the *San Carlos* 110 days to arrive in port. By that time, there was only one crewmember on deck capable of lowering the anchor! One might note that, in a modern sailing vessel, one could hope to make the journey in a week.

The remaining crews from both ships carried their sick and dying ashore, thus creating one of San Diego's lesser-celebrated landmarks – *La Punta de los Muertos*, or Dead Man's Point. The original Point is near the Foot of Market St., though the monument has since been relocated to a site near Seaport Village (at the corner of Pacific Highway and Harbor Drive).

Just as La Punta de los Muertos marks the burial site of many a mariner, it also marks the beginning of the settlement of San Diego.

Portolá and Fr. Serra would eventually meet up with their supply ships, in time to survey their misery. They then set about the task of building a small mission, which would act not only as a hospital but as a defense outpost.

The small outpost barely survived its beginnings. The lack of a dependable source of fresh water was of great concern, even in those early days. The San Diego River (which is now marked by Mission Valley) was either barely potable in the dry season, or a flooding torrent in the wet season.

Even though some accounts dispute the point, it seemed that wood along the coast was sparse. In what might be an historical exaggeration, it was noted that the Indians were enlisted to drag logs down from the mountains. This was only one of many examples of how the Indians were used in the "employ" of the military and missionaries. Thus began the Indians' discontent with the white man's settlements, and the beginning of endless skirmishes.

1774

◆

In an attempt to disengage the Mission San Diego de Alcala from the military presence, Fr. Serra, with only a small guard, moved a few miles inland along the San Diego River. There the Franciscans, with the help of a few Christian Indians, built a new mission.

Mission San Diego de Alcala has gone through several transformations over the years. It was burned down by the Indians in 1775 and rebuilt, then leveled by an earthquake in 1803. Funds were allotted for the Mission to be rebuilt in 1931. Now with an active parish, it remains in a good state of repair (close to Mission Valley).

Bob Covarrubias

1793

◆

The year 1793 marks a turning point in San Diego's history. George Vancouver, aboard his British ship *Discovery*, sailed into San Diego Bay. This was the first foreign ship to do so. Vancouver was under orders to survey the coastline and ports, and to estimate the strength of Spain's military defenses. His writings, describing San Diego and the Presidio, are somewhat grim:

"...The situation of it is dreary and lonesome, in the midst of a barren uncultivated country...."

He surmised that the Spanish Presidio was "...inferior in the point of situation, regularity and cleanliness...."

But Vancouver noted optimistically:

"With little difficulty San Diego might also be rendered a place of considerable strength, by establishing a small force at the entrance of the port; where, at this time, there were neither works, guns, houses, or other habitations nearer than the presidio, which is at the distance of at least five miles from the port, and where they have only three small pieces of brass cannon."

This painting of the **Lelia Byrd** *by San Diegan Jerry MacMullen captured the action of the moment.*

It seems that the Spanish were suitably impressed by the British captain's visit. They immediately set about building a fortified defense, at a point just inside the entrance to the bay.

It was laid with cobblestones, and so named "Point Guijarros," or cobblestone point.

When the hide ships and other "Yankee Traders" began to sail into San Diego, Point Guijarros took on another name. Apparently, the outgoing vessels would take on some of the cobblestones, and use them for ballast on the return trip to the East Coast, via Cape Horn. The name then became "Ballast Point." As the story goes, when the ships anchored in Boston Harbor, the stones were thrown overboard. A great quantity of those stones then accumulated and, when the Boston tidelands were developed, they used the cobblestones to pave the adjacent streets.

San Diego has a long and impressive history as a military base. Though it would mobilize for two world wars, and partake in many international crises, only once would it fire its artillery at short range.

In this particular incident, the "enemy" was the American brig *Lelia Byrd*. She had sailed into San Diego in 1803, in hopes of smuggling out a shipload of sea-otter furs. The high-priced furs had been confiscated from the last Yankee vessel, which had attempted to sneak out of port with the bounty. The Spanish were determined to control these valuable pelts, and so, after a failed attempt by the sailors of the *Lelia Byrd* to smuggle the furs on board at night, the Spanish readied their guns at Fort Guijarros (Ballast Point). After one warning shot was fired, the second one was launched. The *Lelia Byrd* sustained some damage, but was able to get off a full broadside from her guns aimed at the Spanish fort. An account of the outcome reports:

"Our second broadside seemed to have caused the complete abandonment of their guns, as none were fired afterwards; nor could we see any person sin the fort, excepting a soldier who stood upon the ramparts, waving his hat, as if to desist firing."

Courtesy of San Diego Historical Society, Photograph Collection

▼

Though this photo of Ballast Point was taken 82 years after the so-called Battle of San Diego, the area remained quite undeveloped well into the 20th Century.

A replica of the Pilgrim can be seen along California's coastal waters today. Dana first described the Pilgrim as "a remarkably fast sailer, having been built for the smuggling trade."

The 87' brig still runs swiftly before the wind, though she now sails for purposes of education. She hails from Dana Point, where the Orange County Marine Institute offers tours, lectures and plays for people of all ages and interests, as well as ocean-going training sails.

Chapter Two

That's Right My Boys, Never Say Die!

1835

◆

San Diego was becoming an increasingly busy port in the early 1800's with the arrival of English, Russian, French, American and Spanish ships seeking to establish trading outposts. Local sea-otter furs, cow hides and tallow proved to be precious commodities. Merchant ships also needed a safe harbor to call into, to replenish their water and supplies.

Courtesy of
San Diego Historical Society,
Ticor Collection

Among all the visiting ships, there was one ship made notorious by an able-bodied seaman who hailed from Harvard! With a lawyer's eye for detail and a writer's predilection for story-telling, he meticulously recorded the life of a sailor in those days, the ports they called into, and the daily routine on board.

Though this photo was taken in 1910, it reflects the placid nature of La Playa, which was still largely undeveloped. The dirt-rutted road of Rosecrans Street is visible near the water's edge. The house in the foreground is still in existence today. Once owned by the Fletcher family, this house perhaps best represents the Fletchers' long-standing involvement in the development of San Diego.

Richard Henry Dana shipped out at the age of twenty, aboard the Yankee brig *Pilgrim*. His ship sailed out of Boston Harbor, bound for California. Dana later returned to Boston, completed his studies at Harvard and became a lawyer. It was during this period that Dana penned his experiences of life at sea in *Two Years Before the Mast*.

Dana's writings, are intriguing for their descriptions of various ports, including San Diego, and the curious business of drying hides in preparation for their long sea voyage.

Concerning a sailor's life, Dana writes:

"Yet a sailor's life is at best but a mixture of a little good with much evil, and a little pleasure with much pain. The beautiful is linked with the revolting, the sublime with the commonplace, and the solemn with the ludicrous."

Upon entering San Diego in 1835, Dana reports:

"At sunset on the second day, we had a large and well wooded headland directly before us, behind which lay the little harbor of San Diego....A chain of high hills, beginning at the point [Point Loma], protected the harbor on the north and west, and ran off into the interior as far as the eye could reach. On the other sides, the land was low, and green, but without trees. The entrance is so narrow as to admit but one vessel at a time, the current [is] swift, and the channel runs so near to a low stony point [Ballast Point] that the ship's sides appeared almost to touch it....There was no town in sight....

"For landing and taking on board hides, San Diego is decidedly the best place in California. The harbor is small and land-locked; there is no surf; the vessels lie within a cable's length [approximately six hundred feet] of the beach; and the beach itself is smooth, hard sand, without rocks or stones. For these reasons, it is used by all the vessels in the trade, as a depot..."

Dana goes on to record, with painstaking accuracy, the process of curing and loading the hides onto the ship. He describes their soaking in brine, thus "pickling" the hides; the staking of the hides in order to cut away the unusable parts; then the cleaning and drying. They were stowed in the hide houses overnight, then taken out in the morning to be salted, scraped, cleaned, dried, beaten and stowed again. They would lie in the hide houses until their final loading on board the ship.

The hide houses of which Dana writes were located in La Playa. Today, the sandy beach rests idly, with the same placid waters lapping against the shoreline. One of the most beautiful views of San Diego Bay can be secured from this cove, or from its close neighbor, the San Diego Yacht Club. Also sharing the cove at La Playa is the Southwestern Yacht Club.

▼

Camouflaged by a sea of masts, the San Diego Yacht Club rests comfortably in La Playa. Always witness to a changing city skyline, the club remains a stalwart fixture with proud remembrances of the past, while facing a challenging future.

Dale Frost, Port of San Diego

1846

◆

California was increasingly uneasy under Mexican rule (independence from Spain had been achieved in 1821). As the movement of foreign ships between ports became more frequent, Mexico's instability and vulnerability became evident.

When the Americans began to move their military forces westward, American warships mobilized along the West Coast. In 1846, the sloop-of-war U.S.S. *Cyane* sailed down from Monterey and secured the port of San Diego. They raised the Stars & Stripes with little resistance.

Among the passengers on board *Cyane* was the illustrious Kit Carson. Though reportedly seasick at the time, Carson was considered the hero of the Battle of San Pasqual, fought near San Diego in December 1846.

The year 1847 marked the end of Mexican rule, and by 1848, California was ceded to the United States.

In the ensuing years, the bay of San Diego would be a port of call for a long list of gallant vessels. Among them would be three- and four-masted schooners, brigs and brigantines, barks and barkentines and fully-rigged ships. Their trades would range from lumber schooners, cargo and whaling ships, to military vessels.

▼

On July 29, 1846, Lt. Stephen C. Rowan from the U.S.S. Cyane was the first to raise the United States flag in Southern California. It was not long after that the Mexicans revolted against the occupation and tore down the flag.

A local sailmaker from La Playa, Albert Smith, climbed up the flagpole and nailed another American flag to the pole. It stood there until the Old Town fire in 1872.

Courtesy of San Diego Historical Society, Ticor Collection

1851

◆

Bob Covarrubias

▶

The Californian was built in 1983/4, over a period of eleven months at San Diego's Spanish Landing, just off of North Harbor Drive (across from The San Diego International Airport).

The arena was so consistently full of curious spectators that lectures were given concerning all phases of construction. Steve Christman, executive director of the Nautical Heritage Society, described the project at hand.

A magnificent example of a mid-nineteenth century sailing vessel can be seen on San Diego waters today. Under the auspices of the Nautical Heritage Society (located in Dana Point), and with the enthusiastic assistance of sailors, expert designers and skillful maritime craftsmen, the 145-foot topsail schooner *Californian* now sails the western seaboard.

Dale Frost, Port of San Diego

Her design is based on the ill-fated Revenue Cutter *C.W. Lawrence*, which was celebrated as the swiftest and most elegant vessel of her time. Her speed was an important function of her design, for the class of Revenue Cutters played an important role in our nation's early maritime history. As a forerunner of today's U.S. Coast Guard, the Cutters were enlisted to protect coastal waters from the activities of privateers, slavers, opium traders and smugglers. The Cutters also enforced revenue and customs laws, and aided vessels in distress.

◀

Each phase of the project required absolute precision. To that end, the master builder gathered the finest shipwrights and craftsmen available from the U.S. and from other countries where such skills are revered.

The *C.W. Lawrence* was lost in 1851, just south of San Francisco Bay, as she attempted to lay off the coast in heavy seas. After her mooring cable broke, she shipped water, and was unable to make way against the tumultuous seas. The *Lawrence* foundered, she was driven ashore and wrecked.

Today, the *Californian* sails the coast proudly, as the state of California's Official Tall Ship. Not only does she bring to life an earlier era, but she offers to youths who train aboard her, or to any seasoned sailor, a nautical experience which reaches deep into our nautical past. Though the ports themselves have changed remarkably, the sea and the wind surrounding them have not.

Dale Frost, Port of San Diego

Jayforth Hazell used the traditional tools of a caulking mallet and iron to caulk the ship's hull with oakum. Jayforth is considered to be in the class of true shipwrights, having the skill to build a boat from the keel up. Hailing from Bequia, Jayforth learned his trade as a young boy while assisting in building traditional schooners on the beach near his home.

Bob Covarrubias

Baron Thomas's lifelong love and expertise is in the area of traditional ship's carpentry. As a master craftsman, he was called upon to hand-craft all the blocks, dead eyes and the six gun carriages on board. These are just a few of his many skills. On site at the Californian, Baron cut out the brackets for the gun carriages, which supported six-pound bronze cannons. Baron skillfully carries on the seafaring tradition of his family in San Diego.

Dale Frost, Port of San Diego

Master builder Melbourne Smith applies his delicate brush strokes with great care to the stern of the Californian.

Dale Frost, Port of San Diego

▲

Melbourne drives the last spike into the ship's hull. The spike is called the "whiskey plank spike" because tradition calls for a round or two of whiskey, signifying a job well done.

Melbourne Smith, designer and builder of the Californian, could well be considered the epitome of the Renaissance man. His maritime knowledge and skills are broad indeed. After running away to sea at the age of 14, Mr. Smith has spent a lifetime either sailing on ships, designing, building or re-building sailing vessels; or with paint brush and easel in hand, preserving their images on canvas.

Dale Frost

▲

With the ship built and ready to be launched, the mud and sand bottom off Spanish Landing proved to be too soft. The ship had to be driven along the busy thoroughfare on Harbor Drive to a new launching sight at the Coast Guard Station on Harbor Island, where her hull finally met seawater.

▶

The Tall Ship Californian sails in Pacific waters with a full schedule of educational programs. She imparts to the young people who train on board her the traditional maritime values of teamwork, self-reliance and discipline.

Bob Covarrubias

It might only be a small and curious detail in San Diego's sailing history that in the mid-1850's, the Pacific Pioneer Yacht Club was formed in San Diego. Consider the town of San Diego, then located in Old Town, which in the 1860's struggled to maintain a population of 700! The gold rush in northern California had lured some locals north, while the military presence dwindled after California had been secured from Mexico.

Courtesy of San Diego Historical Society, Ticor Collection

This photo, dated 1869, shows the substantial distance from Old Town to the bay. Notice the ship's mast at the center of the town square attempting to acknowledge the town's position.

Old Town was set back from the bay water by some miles and did not seem particularly inviting to visitors. One energetic speculator, William Heath Davis, came to town and tried to move the small settlement closer to the harbor. A substantial investment was made in the new site: houses, stores, barracks and a hotel were built. Within two years it was a ghost town. Davis's plan would be captioned in history as "Davis's Folly."

A Pioneer's Yacht Club it must have been. It seems to have managed only one successful regatta, before fading out of existence. Yet the *San Diego Herald* recorded the event of April 10, 1852, with quite an enthusiastic tone:

"...the streets were crowded with lovely ladies and gentlemen decked out in their finery. The streets were crowded with carriages, and excitement was the order of the day. An Indian sac-race was an added attraction..."

There were some visitors who did not share the local enthusiasm for the San Diego of that era. One traveler to Old Town summed up his impressions as he neared the central plaza:

Stephen Simpson

The William Heath Davis House was one of the first homes built in Davis's New Town. It is the oldest surviving structure in the area. This prefabricated house was shipped from the East Coast to California around Cape Horn. Originally constructed at State and Market streets in 1850, it is now located at 410 Island Avenue in the Gaslamp Quarter.

"Of all the dilapidated, miserable looking places I had ever seen, this was the worst...."

It would be hard to envision a yacht club burgeoning under these circumstances. Yacht racing, however, was indeed flourishing in other, more prosperous environments.

America's Cup History
1851

In 1851, the British hosted a yacht race as part of their Great Exhibition. The Exhibition was essentially a platform for introducing industrial and agricultural equipment sent from various foreign markets. The Americans sent over a sampling of many products; among them was the sleek schooner *America*.

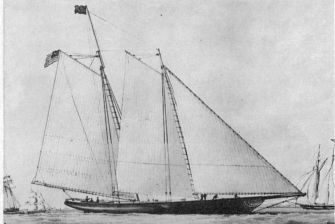

Rosenfeld Collection, Mystic Seaport Museum

America turned up a few British noses to be sure; her design was uniquely American. But the fledgling yacht soundly defeated sixteen of Britain's finest schooners and cutters in the regatta sailed around the Isle of Wight. The prize for the yacht race, offered by the Royal Yacht Squadron, was the Hundred Guineas Cup (reflecting its cost). After *America's* victory, the cup would be re-named the "America's Cup."

In 1857, the owners of *America* transferred the Cup to the New York Yacht Club under a Deed of Gift, which read:

"Any organized yacht club of any foreign country shall always be entitled, through any one or more of its members, to claim the right of sailing a match for this cup with any yacht or other vessel of no less than 30 or more than 200 tons, measured by the custom house rule of the country to which the vessel belongs. It is to be distinctly understood that the cup is to be the property of the club, and not of the members thereof, or owners of the vessel winning it in the match, and that the conditions of keeping it open to be sailed for by yacht clubs of all foreign countries, upon the terms above laid down, shall forever attach to it, thus making it perpetually a challenge cup for friendly competition between foreign countries."

The terms of the Deed of Gift have been challenged and altered over the years, but the initial spirit of competition has been carefully preserved.

The America's Cup represents the pinnacle of yachting competition. Skippers, sailors, designers, builders and entrepreneurs, all share their expertise in the hope of attaining this magnificent symbol of excellence.

Bob Covarrubias

The Goliah was the first side-wheeler to dock in San Diego harbor in 1851. Another famous steamer was the Orizaba, which brought most of the new residents to San Diego in the early years. While the steamers were the main form of transportation before the railroads were built, they did not boast of many comforts. Their staterooms were reportedly "small and stuffy," with no more than 5' 10" of headroom.

Chapter Three

Heaven on Earth

1851

◆

The arrival of the side-wheeler *Goliah* in 1851 heralded the beginning of regular steamship service between San Diego and San Francisco. The fragile link between the small and dusty Old Town and greater commerical centers was strengthened.

Many of San Diego's most illustrious characters arrived on the side-wheelers. On board the steamer *Northerner* was Lt. George Horatio Derby, a U.S. topographical engineer. Lt. Derby was sent from Washington "to dam the San Diego River." He apparently "damned" it several times for its obstinate nature. The attempt was made in the 1850's to divert the flow of water from the San Diego River to *"False Bay"* (Mission Bay) in an effort to avoid further silting in San Diego harbor. The "Derby Dyke" was operable until the mid-1870's when a flood silted the dyke.

Bay of San Diego.   Slocum Studio.

Courtesy of
San Diego Historical Society,
Ticor Collection

▲

This overall view of San Diego harbor in 1887 shows its general character-istics as a harbor suitable for shipping. Over the years navigational charts would become more precise, and by the 1890's dredging was begun in order to keep the shipping channel free of silt.

Lt. Derby would leave a greater imprint on local history as a writer for the *San Diego Herald*. Writing under the pen name "John Phoenix," and later, "Squibob," Lt. Derby sketched early California portraitures with a wonderfully humorous pen.

Upon his arrival in San Diego in 1853, Lt. Derby reported his first impressions after disembarking from the *Northerner* at La Playa:

"Then there is the Ocean House and a store marked Gardiner & Bleeker, the inside of which nothing could be bleeker for there's nothing in it, and an odd-looking little building on stilts out in the water where a savant named Sabot, in the employ of the U.S. Engineers, makes mysterious obser-vations on the tide. These with three other small unoccupied buildings, a fence and a graveyard constitute all the `improve-ments' that have been made at the Playa. The ruins of two old hide-houses, immortalized by Dana in his *Two Years Before the Mast*, are still standing, one bearing the weather-beaten name of Tasso. We examined these houses and got well bitten by fleas for our trouble."

1855

◆

Increasing sea traffic generated a need for a dependable navigation aid to help guide ships around Point Loma and into port. The first lighthouse was completed in 1855; it still stands today, atop the most southerly tip of Point Loma (it is now a part of Cabrillo National Monument). The lighthouse rests on a promontory 422 feet above sea level. Its elevation proved to be the cause of its demise. On many foggy San Diego days (and nights), it could not be seen through the thick blanket of mist. It was replaced in 1890 by a lighthouse situated on Ballast Point. A supplemental lighthouse was erected in 1891, on the western side of Point Loma.

From the 1850's and well into the 1880's, whaling ships were a common sight in San Diego Bay. Sailors from ships returning to the East Coast recounted tales of seeing large schools of whales inside the harbor (mainly from December to

➤

The 1855 lighthouse still stands today atop Point Loma.

As part of Cabrillo National Monument, surveyors of history can catch a glimpse of how the lighthouse keepers lived in those early days. The Israel family lived at the lighthouse from 1871 to 1891. They must have been a robust clan indeed. Isolation was one of the main ingredients of the job. The family had to travel quite a distance over Point Loma to reach the nearest settlement for supplies.

Bob Covarrubias

March as the whales headed south to their breeding grounds in Mexico). Upon hearing the stories, the East Coast whaling ships readied themselves for the long and hazardous voyage around Cape Horn.

At certain times of the year, sailing ships arriving in San Diego Bay would find so many whales that they presented a navigational hazard. The whales, moving in large pods, not only posed a hazard to the sailing ships, but they were a sizable inconvenience to anyone trying to row from Ballast Point to North Island. Max Miller, in his classic book on San Diego Bay, *Harbor of the Sun*, recounted how the shore people of the whaling stations (on the Point Loma side) would attempt to row across the main channel in an effort to get fresh water from "Whaler's Spring" on North Island. It often necessitated waiting until the enormous mammals had cleared the entrance.

Bob Covarrubias

A second lighthouse was built in 1891 on the west side of Point Loma.

The Ballast Point Lighthouse was erected as a replacement for the Old Point Loma Lighthouse in 1890.

Courtesy of San Diego Historical Society, Ticor Collection

At the height of the whalers' activities in San Diego, 55,000 gallons of whale oil were produced in one year.

Today, the whales are protected in local waters, and are only pursued by whale watchers straining to catch a glimpse of these beautifully graceful creatures. Every once in a while, a calf strays away from its cow, and harbor waters are again ruffled by the powerful flukes of the gray whale.

The Charles W. Morgan is the last wooden whaling ship in America. In her berth at the Mystic Seaport Museum in Mystic, Connecticut, she captures the spotlight with her long seagoing history. Measuring 111' from stem to stern, she is a good example of the whaling ship of her day. With 37 voyages to her credit, spanning 80 years of sailing, the whaling bark crossed more miles of ocean, and made more profits for her owners, than any other whaleship on record. Life at sea, as Dana recounted, was full of hardship and tedium, though not without its high seas adventures.

◀

Neva Sullaway

►

Every year the California Gray Whales can be seen gliding south along the coast on their way to their breeding grounds in Baja.

Bob Covarrubias

1867

◆

The man who would become known as the "Father of San Diego" arrived in 1867, on board the small steamer *Pacific*. Alonzo E. Horton had been so inspired by a lecture he attended in San Francisco concerning the coastal ports of California, that he boarded the steamer with the dream of building a town in San Diego. The lecture promoted San Diego as having the healthiest of climates, with one of the finest natural harbors in the world.

This view of San Diego in 1874 reflects Horton's singular vision. The new wharf was built in 1868 and it would be the key to New Town's development. Note the windmills near the foreshore for drawing water from wells.

Courtesy of San Diego Historical Society, Ticor Collection

"Father Horton" is pictured in his later years at the age of 93. Still looking quite robust, Horton broke ground for the Elks Hall. Horton passed away three years later (1909) at the age of 96. Even though he gave so much of his life and spirit to San Diego, he died virtually penniless.

Courtesy of San Diego Historical Society, Photograph Collection

Horton stepped off the *Pacific* at what is now the foot of Market Street. While waiting for the buckboard to take him and other passengers to Old Town (three miles to the northeast), Horton sauntered up a slope which gave him a clear view, not only of the bay, but of the Los Coronados Islands looming far off on the horizon. Later, he remarked:

"I thought San Diego must be a Heaven on Earth, if it was all as fine as that. It seemed to me the best spot for building a city I ever saw."

At fifty-four years of age, Horton proved to be an indefatigable visionary, bringing to San Diego his energy, perseverance and entrepreneurial background. All these qualities were powerfully combined with the instincts of a natural salesman. After selling his furniture business in San Francisco, Horton brought his capital assets as well.

Horton has been described as standing five-feet ten-inches tall, presenting an impressive stature, while maintaining a quiet, reserved nature. He was not so much a self-promoter as he was fully dedicated to the idea of building the new San Diego.

Horton recognized the land along the harbor as being the natural site for "New Town." After pressing the local County Clerk into calling an election for a new board of Trustees (the governing body at the time), Horton soon found elected favorable supporters for his land purchases. The notice for the land auction was posted. Horton bid what was considered a ridiculously excessive price for the flea-ridden, semi-desert terrain and purchased 960 acres at an average cost of twenty-seven and a half cents an acre!

In 1895 Horton deeded the last of his holdings to the City of San Diego. He sold the Plaza (which stood across from the Horton House) for $10,000. This amount was to be paid at the rate of $100 a month until 1903. While the city wagered a potential profit, Horton outlived all their expectations and collected the full amount.

Courtesy of San Diego Historical Society, Ticor Collection

Today, the U.S. Grant Hotel is on the prior site of the Horton House. With equally grand architecture and furnishings, it recalls the elegance of the Victorian period.

Stephen Simpson

Courtesy of San Diego Historical Society, Ticor Collection

The Horton House had its gala opening in 1870. With one hundred rooms furnished in the grandest style of the times, the hotel was Horton's showcase attraction. It proved to be one of many of Horton's successful projects, which attracted visitors and new businesses to San Diego.

Horton succeeded where William Heath Davis had earlier failed. A new wharf was built in 1868 at the foot of Fifth Street (now the area seaward of the Convention Center). The new wharf offered a disembarkation point for passengers (they no longer had to be carried ashore by sailors), and an offloading dock for commercial vessels.

San Diego would begin to grow under the tutelage of "Father Horton." He continued to make his sea voyages to San Francisco, touting San Diego's climate not only as healthful, but as a curative for all sorts of ills.

1869

◆

In 1869, the *San Diego Union* announced:

"People are coming here by the hundreds, by steamer, by stage, and by private conveyance....From a place of no importance...we now have a city of 3,000 inhabitants....Every steamer from San Francisco averages 200 passengers for San Diego."

Vast improvements came with the growing population. A new school was built, and the water system was improved. The arrival of the telegraph, telephone and electricity would all contribute to the burgeoning New Town. A fire in Old Town in 1872 virtually assured the survival of New Town. No longer rivals, the residents of Old Town gradually moved closer to San Diego's new center.

This 1876 view of San Diego's Fifth Street (south of Broadway) reflects the rapid expansion of the 1870's.

Courtesy of San Diego Historical Society, Ticor Collection

San Diego would know times of bust and times of boom. This particular era experienced two remarkable booms; one occurred in 1871-1873, after gold was discovered in Julian, a nearby mountain town. The second occurred in 1886-1888, when the railroad finally arrived in San Diego. The atmosphere must have been buoyant indeed; there was talk of creating a yacht club.

1886

◆

The rather convoluted story of the new yacht club really begins with the creation of the San Diego Rowing Club in 1886. Several renditions of the first meeting (which took place at Horton's Hall, with 55 people present) are available. Suffice it to say, the yacht club got under way. The account, as rendered by Charles La Dow, one of the San Diego Yacht Club historians, introduces names that would be instrumental in developing the club. These same people would also form the early foundations for the maritime city of San Diego.

Courtesy of San Diego Historical Society, Ticor Collection

The Jessop family has a long history in San Diego, dating back to the arrival of Joseph and Mary Jessop in 1890. It was not long before Joseph Jessop opened J. Jessop & Sons Jewelers in 1893.

With five sons to carry on the family business, J. Jessop & Sons Jewelers would eventually have ten stores in the San Diego area.

The list of early yacht club members includes: U.S. Grant Jr. (son of President U.S. Grant), Dr. F. R. Burnham (a physician and surgeon who became active in civic affairs as well as business), L.A. Blockman (banker and industrialist), Dr. Fred Baker (who was instrumental in the founding of Scripps Institution of Oceanography), and Alonzo de Jessop (whose family name would become synonymous with the San Diego Yacht Club).

Heaven on Earth

These men, driven by the early pioneer spirit, would share with Horton the promise of a maritime city. The development of the natural harbor breathed life into the struggling town center. It was the focus for all transportation and trade. It would spawn a fishing and ship-building industry, naval station and aircraft manufacturing. Through careful planning, it would eventually form the hub of San Diego's recreation and tourist attractions.

Early San Diego photographs capture the many activities of the bustling harbor.

◄ *These photos dated 1900, courtesy of the San Diego Maritime Museum, capture the relaxing pose of Alonzo de Jessop at the helm. Alonzo was most likely sailing aboard a chartered fishing vessel, which was made available by the Portuguese and Italian fishermen who did not fish on Saturdays or Sundays, in strict observance of their religion.*

▼ *This casual afternoon sail in 1900 finds brother Armand Jessop (front left), Miss Bushell (front right), and Violet Jessop seated next to Alonzo at the helm, enjoying an uncrowded sail on the bay.*

▼
The Santa Fe Wharf was built in 1888 by the Spreckels Brothers' Commercial Company. Its express purpose was for handling heavy cargoes such as coal, cement and other bulk commodities.

Courtesy of San Diego Historical Society, Ticor Collection

▲

This classic 1886 photo from the San Diego Historical Society's Ticor Collection reflects the working San Diego waterfront. The railroad had arrived in 1885, bringing with it more residents and business opportunities. The lumber in the foreground reminds the viewer that wood was scarce in San Diego and had to be imported. The sailing ships remained the vital link for transportation and trade until the 1900's when the coming of the diesel engine began to replace sail and steam power.

This location today is at the foot of Fourth Street where you will find the old railroad tracks before entering the Embarcadero Marina Park.

Courtesy of San Diego Historical Society, Ticor Collection

The busy wharves of the 1880's left a lasting impression on San Diego.

Courtesy of San Diego Historical Society, Photograph Collection

The Chinese initially made their way south from San Francisco to work on the California Southern Railway, being built from National City and heading north. In the 1870's, it was not uncommon to see Chinese junks, or small, flat-bottomed sampans, sweeping the bay with fine-mesh seines imported from China. Junks were often seen heading out to the kelp beds to fish. The Chinese sold larger fish such as smelt and mullet door to door. Fish that were too small to sell would be dried and preserved, and eventually exported to China. Though the Chinese boats might have appeared foreign to San Diego waters, they were, in fact, built in San Diego and considered quite seaworthy, fast and maneuverable. In the 1890's, one-third of all the fishermen in California were Chinese.

An area of ill repute called the "Stingaree" flourished in the late 1800's as Cape Horners, railroad boomers and the wild west men came to town.

The Seamen's Rest was located at the foot of West Market, placing it just off the Santa Fe Wharf – a convenient first stop for a thirsty sailor.

Those were bawdy times, with the number of saloons at 71, far outnumbering any other enterprise in San Diego. Though not sailors, men like Wyatt Earp were seen in this part of town. Shoot-outs were a common occurrence in the Stingaree.

Courtesy of San Diego Historical Society, Ticor Collection

In the days before the Navy acquired North Island (1921), the land was largely vacant. However, the northern tip of North Island provided an accessible area for hauling ships for repair work. There the four-masted schooner Americana prepared for another sailing season.

Courtesy of San Diego Historical Society, Ticor Collection

The historic sloop
Butcher Boy *tried to
edge to windward of
the well-canvassed*
Detroit *in the 1905
Lipton Cup match race.*

Butcher Boy *was built
in 1902 by Manuel
Goularte at his
boatyard at the foot of
B Street. Framed in
oak, planked with
cedar, and fastened
with copper nails,*
Butcher Boy *was
every bit the sturdy
vessel she was
modelled after.*

Chapter Four

Down the Coronado Roads

1880's

◆

The Hotel del Coronado appeared as the backdrop for many early photographs which featured recreational boating. Much of San Diego's early "yachting" included going over to the hotel's boathouse (now the Chart House Restaurant) by ferry, and renting a Cat Boat for the afternoon.

Residing majestically near the water's edge, the Hotel del Coronado offers a glorious view of the Pacific. The Hotel del Coronado was completed in 1888, chiefly through the investment efforts of E.S. Babcock and H.L. Story. The hotel would not only become known as the "Grand Dame" of Victorian resort hotels, but would also become something of a celebrity in its own right. Among those who came to enjoy the pleasant climate were royalty, presidents, educators, musicians, artists, high-ranking military officers, statesmen, corporate heads, aviators, scientists, and not least among them – the movie stars. More than sixty-five movies have been shot on location at the "Del."

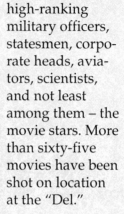

Courtesy of San Diego Historical Society, UnionTribune Collection

▼

After the gala opening of the Hotel del Coronado in 1888, the San Diego Union *captured the excitement of the moment with front page headlines:*

"A Hotel That is Surpassed by None in the World, Like Unto an Old Norman Castle."

▲

This map of San Diego, which was made for the Panama California Exposition of 1915, graphically delineates the San Diego area at that time. Note the location of the Hotel del Coronado and Coronado's Tent City in relation to San Diego (with no bridge to span the distance).

Courtesy of
San Diego Historical Society,
Photograph Collection

➤

This 1939 photo, courtesy of the Scripps Institution of Oceanography Archives, UCSD, recalls the rigors of early research expeditions. On board Scripps sailing ship is pioneer oceanographer Roger Revelle (second from left). Revelle is highly regarded not only for his sixty-year involvement with Scripps Institution, but also for his involvement in the establishment of the University of California campus at La Jolla.

Revelle arrived at Scripps in 1931 as a geology graduate student. For nearly three decades, Revelle was part of deep-sea explorations, whose discoveries added greatly to our knowledge of the underwater world.

In 1990, Roger Revelle (at 81 years of age) received the National Medal of Science, which reflected not only his investigations into complex scientific phenomena, but the extraordinarily broad range of his creative and intellectual processes.

▼

This 1887 photo of the Coronado Boathouse and Bathhouse points up several interesting features concerning Coronado. Firstly, the building itself reflects the stunning Victorian style of architecture. Secondly, the Boathouse provided a platform from which to study the marine environment. Dr. Fred Baker, aside from being an avid sailor, was a collector of seashells and marine specimens. It was from the Coronado Boathouse that he and William Ritter (professor of zoology from UC Berkeley) began to gather information from local waters with the hope of someday having a marine biological station in the vicinity. Through the collective efforts of many people, most notably E.W. Scripps, an appropriate sight in La Jolla was eventually chosen, and the world-renowned Scripps Institution of Oceanography came into being.

Courtesy of San Diego Historical Society, Union Tribune Collection

All this might have been a bit more than Babcock and Story envisioned when they first purchased the land, the sole inhabitants of which were rabbits, squirrels and rattlesnakes ranging over the scrub land.

San Diego's history was about to be altered again, as the stately schooner *Lurline* rounded Point Loma. On board was John D. Spreckels, the son of Claus Spreckels, the "Sugar King" of Hawaii and San Francisco. Though the millionaire's son called into port only to restock his supplies, he would end up becoming a pivotal influence in San Diego.

Spreckels saw the boom town potential, and immediately began a long list of investments and acquisitions. He built a wharf and coal storage bunkers at the foot of Broadway, and pulled the hub of town away from Fifth Street to Broadway by erecting some impressive buildings which rivaled Horton's.

Courtesy of San Diego Historical Society, Ticor Collection

Eventually Spreckels would buy out the Hotel Del Coronado and most of the holdings of Babcock and Story. They included the streetcar system, the ferries, and the water system. Spreckels also owned two daily newspapers, some real estate, and a score of other businesses in town.

Courtesy of San Diego HistoricalSociety, Photograph Collection

1900's

◆

At the turn of the century, early yachting events came under the title of "Water Carnivals." They were casual, fun get-togethers in which boats of almost any description were sailed in informal races.

Struggling yacht clubs of the early 1900's were a curious mix of members, club names and shifting locations. The San Diego Yacht Club, which at one time was a part of the Corinthian Yacht Club, went through many transitions before finding its place of honor in La Playa.

Other yacht clubs formed in different locations around the harbor. The Chula Vista Yacht Club, located in the South Bay

At first a rival yacht club, the Corinthian would eventually merge with the San Diego Yacht Club in 1905. The Corinthian burgee, which was adopted by the San Diego Yacht Club, is still flown today.

➤

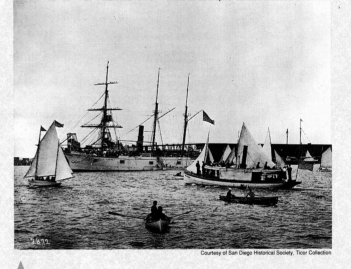

Courtesy of San Diego Historical Society, Ticor Collection

▲

The Water Carnival held in San Diego in May 1901 attracted quite a collection of small craft. The local ferry General De Russy was most likely acting as both a spectator boat and the committee boat. The large naval ship in the background attests to the early presence of the Navy in San Diego. After the Spanish-American War (1898), the movement of naval vessels in and out of San Diego Bay was a common sight.

Courtesy of Port of San Diego

➤

The Star Boathouse and Rowing Club (the building between the two wharves) were located at the foot of Fifth Street. The inception of the Rowing Club provided the impetus for creating a yacht club as well.

At the end of the right pier there is a sign: "Boats to Let," for yachting in the late 1800's was comprised mostly of chartering small boats.

Courtesy of
San Diego Historical Society,
Ticor Collection

Courtesy of
San Diego Historical Society.
Ticor Collection

(at the foot of J Street), had a vigorous beginning. Regattas dating back as early as 1889 have been noted. Early club membership was made up of "gentleman farmers" who hailed from the local lemon growing area of Chula Vista. The club proved to be the social link between farmers and city residents well to the north.

The development of the young club weathered a few setbacks in the form of floods, which caused serious damage in the southern basin. The Chula Vista Yacht Club, however, would achieve recognition with its unique class of one-designs; the 27-foot Chula Vista One-Design was a popular boat in its day.

As the SDYC vied for various positions around the bay, the Silvergate ferry provided an interesting interlude. The first propeller-driven double-ender on the coast, she lacked directional stability and had a habit of taking out every dock and pier in her path! She retired early and was used as a dance pavilion (the Floating Casino) before becoming the SDYC clubhouse from 1910 -1914.

The SDYC travails would not be solved until the new clubhouse, first built on Coronado at the end of Tent City, was floated over to its present site at La Playa in 1934. It was a long and arduous journey, spanning more than forty years!

Finally, the San Diego Yacht Club had a home; it stood until 1963, when the present clubhouse was built in its place.

Courtesy of San Diego Yacht Club

Courtesy of San Diego Historical Society, Union Tribune Collection

John Willett and Frank Roseman, both founding members of the San Diego Tall Ship Society, have pursued the history of the Chula Vista One-Design. This picturesque and nicely designed 27' boat was well-adapted to South Bay waters. Designed and built by Clem Stose, it was the largest one-design boat on the Pacific Coast at that time.

Courtesy of John Willett

This 1910 photo shows the first Chula Vista Yacht Club (perched at the end of the pier). The two young ladies pictured are Muriel Rogers with her cousin May Coy. After the floods in 1916 and the late 1920's had wreaked havoc on the bay, the CVYC was dismantled (1934) and taken 250 miles south to Scammons Lagoon in Baja.

The revitalized Chula Vista Marina offers a unique and relaxing South Bay setting for sailing, as well as many other recreational pursuits. The Chula Vista Yacht Club (next to Jake's Restaurant) has a brand new facility in the Marina, which offers year 'round sailing and social events.

Stephen Simpson

1904

◆

The year 1903 marked an auspicious occasion not only for the San Diego Yacht Club but for yachting in Southern California. Outgoing Corinthian Commodore Blockman wrote a letter to Sir Thomas Lipton (who would head five America's Cup campaigns), asking if Lipton's name could be used on a trophy for area competition. Sir Thomas Lipton responded graciously by sending the 32-inch silver Lipton Cup to San Diego.

Perhaps better known today as having built the Lipton Tea empire, Sir Thomas Lipton was considered one of the best sportsmen of his time. Lipton suffered five America's Cup defeats, spanning thirty years (1899 through 1929), which cost him millions of dollars. But the stubborn Scotch-Irishman kept coming back to the States promising to "lift the Auld Mug" for England.

Sir Thomas Lipton became a lifelong friend of the Jessop family. Alonzo Jessop (left) invited Sir Thomas Lipton to San Diego, which Sir Thomas visited as his guest in 1913.

This event inspired renewed enthusiasm in the San Diego Yacht Club. A group of individuals got together and formed a syndicate with the hope of obtaining a yacht for the first Lipton Cup defense in 1904. Nathanael Herreshoff was first approached with the project; with his growing fame as a yacht de-signer/builder, it was hoped that the first defender would be a new Herreshoff boat.

Perhaps a new yacht was too great an investment for the times. After some negotiating, the San Diego Yacht Club decided to bring out from the Great Lakes a boat considered to be the "racing machine" of its day.

Courtesy of Joe Jessop Sr.

The syndicate had managed to scrape together the princely sum of $25 to help bring the 47 1/2-foot sloop *Detroit* to San Diego waters. It was worth it in the end, she proved to be a winner with her sleek hull and impressive sail area. *Detroit* completely dominated the event, which was sailed in the Coronado Roads against three yachts from the South Coast Yacht Club (San Pedro), and little *Estrella* (from the local Corinthian Yacht Club).

When *Detroit* was sold to a South Coast syndicate, they took the Lipton Cup with them. This unfortunate turn for the San Diego Yacht Club did prove fruitful in the end. The Lipton Cup initiated Southern California inter-club yachting competi-tion, which eventuated in the formation of the Southern Cali-fornia Yachting Association.

Although the Lipton Cup went to the South Coast syndicate, the actual races for the Cup were sailed in San Diego until 1921.

The 1905 Lipton Cup race brought a sentimental favorite to the line, San Diego's own *Butcher Boy*. The name of the fine little sloop tells her story. At first *Butcher Boy's* career was that of a working vessel; she transported meat and supplies to ships lying at anchor. The 30' double-ended sloop was really no match for the grander style of *Detroit*, but she had an eye-catching quality and plucky nature.

The story of *Butcher Boy* has always attracted interest in the yacht. *Butcher Boy's* original design was based on a Columbia River salmon boat. She went through many overhauls and many owners.

Courtesy of Dale Frost, Port of San Diego

Chiefly through the recovery efforts of veteran sailor Joe Jessop and Captain Ken Reynard (the man who supervised the restoration of the *Star of India*), *Butcher Boy* was located in the Los Angeles area in 1971 and sailed back down to San Diego.

Butcher Boy is among the last of the harbor workboats in existence, dating from the turn of the century. Now in the hands of the San Diego Maritime Museum, plans are underway to expand the museum's exhibit of classic boats and ships. Currently, the Maritime Museum showcases the bark *Star of India*, the luxury steam yacht *Medea* and the ferryboat *Berkeley*, all of which preserve a nautical history which at one time came dangerously close to being lost. *Butcher Boy*, the Kettenburg P.C. *Wings* and the Monterey fishing boat *Buccaneer* await their premiere at the museum's permanent exhibition of small craft.

America's Cup History
1880-1903

While the San Diego Yacht Club was in its transitional years (merging in 1905 with the Corinthians), the America's Cup prevailed on the East Coast as the preeminent yachting event.

America's Cup contenders would go through several permutations in the time spanning the fifty years to the turn of the century. The challenge of designing yachts for greater speed and strength drew upon the skills of such prominent designers as Edward Burgess and Nathanael Herreshoff.

The boats themselves were getting progressively larger in the mid-1880's as gaff-rigged sloops replaced the valiant schooners.

Rosenfeld Collection,
Mystic Seaport Museum

The early 1900's would witness the extremes of boat length and sail area with the evolution of the Big Class. They were aptly named, for the boats that sailed in this era provided a spectacle unequalled in previous Cup races. Overall length of the boats ranged from 120 feet upwards and sail area was as much as 17,000 square feet. This grandiloquent combination brought viewers en masse to the waters off New York. (The overcrowding of the channels leading into New York Harbor during Cup challenges was one of the reasons for moving the event to Newport, Rhode Island, in 1930.)

The impetus for the Big Class was undoubtedly provided by such wealthy enthusiasts as Sir Thomas Lipton, J.P. Morgan and the Vanderbilts. As financier J.P. Morgan (1837 - 1913) so succinctly put it:

"You can do business with anyone, but you can sail only with a gentleman."

The Big Class represented a moment in yachting history when the race for the America's Cup took on its most dynamic dimensions.

Bob Covarrubias

Local businessman Todd Schwede owns Memory, a classic Herreshoff design modelled after the Herreshoff line of torpedo boats.

This classic photo of Nathanael Herreshoff was taken by James Burton. It is one of his many photos capturing the "Golden Age of Yachting," an era when Herreshoff designs dominated in both the construction of power and sailing craft.

Nathanael Herreshoff earned the most plaudits for his America's Cup boats. He designed and built every America's Cup defender from 1893-1920.

James Burton, Rosenfeld Collection,
Mystic Seaport Museum

The year 1899 saw the first in the line of five of Sir Thomas Lipton's Shamrocks. Her competitor was Columbia, the defender for the Cup in both 1899 and 1901. Designed by Nathanael Herreshoff, Columbia reflected the sheer power and enormity of the Big Class.

James Burton, Rosenfeld Collection, Mystic Seaport Museum

The 1903 defender Reliance was singularly impressive. The largest single-masted racing yacht ever built, she was 144' (length overall) with a sail area of 17,000 sq. feet. Her enormous spinnaker pole was 84' long! There was no expense spared by financier, Cornelius Vanderbilt.

James Herreshoff, Nathanael's eldest brother, provides an interesting excursion back to San Diego's Hotel del Coronado. Apparently, James broke away from the powerful influences of his two brothers, Nat and John (who was blind from the time he was a teenager), for it was those two brothers who formed the Herreshoff Mfg. Co. in Bristol, Rhode Island.

James, with his wife and five children, boarded the train and headed west. Once in San Diego, the family took up residence at the Hotel del Coronado. James was quite an inventor/

Charles Edwin Bolles, Rosenfeld Collection, Mystic Seaport Museum

The 1903 challenger was Lipton's Shamrock III. An interesting side-note of 1903 is that it marked the first time the British utilized a wheel instead of a tiller. Five Shamrocks did not prove to be lucky charms for Lipton.

James Burton, Rosenfeld Collection, Mystic Seaport Museum

James Burton, Rosenfeld Collection,
Mystic Seaport Museum

*This photo by James
Burton, Rosenfeld
Collection, was taken
on board Reliance in
1903. Sixty-four men
were needed for the
herculean tasks of
handling the
enormous sails,
halyards, sheets and
the spinnaker pole.*

*At the wheel is
Charlie Barr, a
renegade skipper who
won three straight
America's Cup
victories – 1899, 1901
and 1903. He
somehow managed to
be the target of "bad
press" with such
words as "cold-
blooded" and
"uncivilized" being
bantered about. At
the bottom of it all
seemed to rest a little
bit of envy for the
Scotsman who came
over to win the Cup
three times for
America.*

*This 1901 photo
of Constitution
provides an example
of the fate of some of
the racing yachts.
Constitution was not
the only yacht to lose
her rig but she most
graphically depicted
the outcome of
pushing the massive
rigs to their
maximum load.
Needless to say,
she did not survive
the eliminations
that year.*

designer in his own right. Each day he would go to the base-
ment of the Del where he worked on his "row-cycle." The
row-cycle was a wooden framed bicycle with hard rubber tires
and handlebars. When the handlebars were inflated, they
acted like oars for propulsion!

James Herreshoff, in fact, had quite a list of inventions to
his credit: the cross-plank design for boat hulls, the sliding seat
for rowboats, mercurial antifouling paint, the thread tension
regulator for the sewing machine, a bicycle driven by a fuel-
burning engine, the tubular marine steam boiler, and the fin
keel for racing yachts – to mention but a few!

James eventually returned to the East Coast with his
family, where he died at the age of 95.

Sailors in San Diego enjoyed a flurry of activity as Alonzo de Jessop managed to assemble nearly thirty yachts for the 1915 Expo Regatta. The Exposition underscored two very important aspects of San Diego at that time – a rejuvenated economy and growing population (nearly 75,000 by 1920).

dewitt '91

Chapter Five

My Topsails are Hoisted, and I Must Out to Sea...

1906

◆

Compared to the yachting activities around the world in the first two decades of the twentieth century, yachting in San Diego was progressing at a moderate pace. It certainly wasn't due to lack of enthusiasm.

Courtesy of San Diego Historical Society, Ticor Collection

After the consolidation of the Corinthian/San Diego Yacht Club, members numbered about 100, with only seventeen sailing boats on the SDYC roster. There was much grumbling and discord when the

As more dock space was required along the waterfront, recreational facilities like the Swimming Tank at the foot of Fifth Street (and the San Diego Yacht Club on D Street – now Broadway) would be required to move.

▼

▲

This 1905 photo of the Santa Fe Wharf tells quite a story. The rise of commerce and industry along the waterfront is evident. In view are the U.S.S. Ranger and the gunboat U.S.S Bennington (white hull – farthest right). Not long after this photo was taken, the Bennington suffered a fatal explosion when her main boiler burst. Reminders of tragedies at sea were ever present.

initiation fee skyrocketed to twenty dollars (from ten dollars in 1902), and the monthly fee jumped from fifty cents to two dollars!

Courtesy of San Diego Historical Society, Ticor Collection

The Lipton Cup was still the main event on the yachting calendar, and 1906 saw a new racing sloop on San Diego waters. The City of San Diego sponsored the construction of *Aeolus*, which Alonzo de Jessop and Frank Wyatt later bought. Locally built at Jensen's boatyard, *Aeolus* arrived on the sailing scene just in time to become the new hometown favorite. Though she was defeated by the South Coast's *Mischief II* in 1906, Aeolus would have quite a successful sailing career.

Courtesy of Joe Jessop Sr.

◄

This 1906 photograph was taken at the launching of Aeolus, the pride of the city of San Diego. The young lady balancing precariously on the foredeck is breaking the customary bottle of champagne over the bow of Aeolus during the christening.

The Junior Program came into being in 1928, when six boys approached Joe Jessop with the idea of having a Junior division in the San Diego Yacht Club. Mr. Jessop was very much in favor of the idea; however, not all the members were. The Junior Program might have had a rocky beginning, but admirably survived to realize some great names in sailing.

Ten clinker-style Cat Boats (also called "Sea Mews") were built in 1918 and raced on the bay. As modest as these little vessels were, they helped produce some fine sailors. Gordon and Al Frost (of Frost Lumber Co.), Bob Town and Ash Bown were among the junior sailors who started out in the Sea Mews. Starlets (which were scaled-down Stars), later took the place of the aging Sea Mews.

The Junior Program thrives today, and can boast quite an impressive list of talented sailors who once served as Junior Commodores: Bob Town, Charlie Rogers, Lynn Woodward, Mark Reynolds, Dan North and Brian Ledbetter. Among the sailing champions from the Junior Program are two names which link San Diego to the America's Cup – Dennis Conner and Malin Burnham.

Courtesy of Joe Jessop Sr.

The three San Diego Yacht Club representatives: Aeolus, Gretchen and Tribly (pictured) would race for ten years against each other, always providing close competition.

This photo taken in 1912 captures the winning skipper Lew B. Harris.

Courtesy of San Diego Historical Society

A 1908 shot aboard Lurline displays a rather dapper crew.

In the arena of larger yachts, John D. Spreckels' graceful schooner *Lurline* would again capture the spotlight as the first finisher in the Honolulu race of 1912. Skippered by Captain Lew B. Harris, the three-time Honolulu Race winner, *Lurline* sailed under the colors of the San Diego Yacht Club.

Courtesy of San Diego Historical Society, Ticor Collection

1908

◆

Though not strictly a "sailing" event, the arrival of the
Great White Fleet in 1908 proved to be a harbinger for the future.
President Theodore Roosevelt sent the impressive naval fleet on
a circumnavigation, as a display of American might and power.
The message the fleet carried with them around the world
was clear.

The fleet, which boasted sixteen battleships, seven destroyers,
and four auxiliary ships all painted white, was the largest naval
fleet ever to undertake such an ambitious tour-de-force. The
ships anchored in the Coronado Roads off the Hotel del
Coronado for three days. Among the harbor activities of 1908, the
Great White Fleet certainly provided the highlight for the year.

Courtesy of San Diego Historical Society, Ticor Collection

1915

◆

The year 1915 again brought San Diego national attention
with the opening of the Panama California Exposition. The
million dollar extravaganza celebrated the opening of the
Panama Canal, with its potential for turning San Diego into a
thriving commercial harbor. By drawing millions of visitors to
San Diego, the Exposition not only promoted its "healthful
climate," but also put on display San Diego's social, agricultural,
commercial and economic gains amidst a beautiful setting.

▲

*This unusual photo,
taken at night in
1908, perhaps best
displays the size of
the Great White
Fleet. The sixteen
battleships were not
able to enter the
harbor due to the
shallow conditions.
Their arrival focused
on the need for
expansive dredging
projects, if San Diego
was to continue
developing as a naval
and commercial port.*

Courtesy of San Diego Historical Society, Photograph Collection

Balboa Park was the site for the 1915 Expo. The 1400-acre park had originally (in 1868) been set aside to be used solely as a public park, without development of any sort. It was to be held in trust forever by the municipal authorities of San Diego.

Today's Balboa Park, a cultural center in a lush garden setting, exists largely through the foresight of George Marston. Marston initially offered $10,000 to the city Park Commission, enabling them to hire Samuel Parsons Jr. & Co. (a prominent landscape architectural firm from New York) to come to San Diego and prepare a comprehensive plan for the Park.

Marston, who started out as the front desk clerk for the Horton House in the 1870's, contributed a great deal to San Diego. He became the successful owner of a department store chain, which would later be sold to the Broadway chain of stores.

In preparation for the Expo, the Park was extensively planted, and many outstanding buildings of a baroque Spanish colonial style were built. This created a unique and very alluring atmosphere for the visitors of 1915 and 1916.

▲

This photograph, as preserved by the San Diego Historical Society, looks more like an artist's surreal rendition of the San Diego of 1915. "The Goat on the Chimney" could represent rural San Diego's retreat in the face of urban expansion.

▼

There were many prominent visitors during the two-year-long Expo. Seated in the "electriquette" wicker cart (with the pigeon on his head!) is Joseph G. Cannon, Speaker of the House of Representatives from 1903 to 1911. Next to him, with a grand smile, is John D. Spreckels. He must have been pleased indeed, seeing one of his dreams realized in the Expo. Spreckels contributed over $100,000 to the event in addition to building the magnificent outdoor Organ Pavilion. It's a wonderful reminder of Spreckels – a man of great vision.

"With the Pigeons" on the Plaza de Panama, San Diego Exposition 1915

Courtesy of San Diego Historical Society, Ticor Collection

Balboa Park continues to serve as a cultural center, attracting many visitors to the Timken Art Gallery, the Aerospace Museum (including the Sports Hall of Fame and Hall of Champions), the Natural History Museum, the Museum of Man, the Reuben H. Fleet Theater & Science Center, the Spanish Village Art Center and Japanese Friendship Garden. The San Diego Historical Society and Museum of Photographic Arts are located in the Park, as well as many other ancillary exhibits. The renowned San Diego Zoo is also within walking distance of the Prado, the Park's "Main Street."

Stephen Simpson

1917

◆

As the war years approached, local yachting suffered with the rest of the country. San Diego yachting went through periods of great activity and decline. Both World War I and World War II called all able-bodied sailors into service.

Then Secretary of the Navy Josephus Daniels paid special tribute to the large number of yachtsmen who joined the war effort. The following excerpt appeared in a 1918 issue of *Country Life* in an article titled "They're in the Navy Now; Yachting Has Gone to the War in Earnest":

"...no recreative form of activity was in a position to be of so much practical value to the Government when we [the United States] entered the war as was yachting. Passing the fact that there were hundreds of yachts which the Navy Department found of inestimable value, we note the thousands of men familiar with navigation, practical seamanship, or boat handling, who were qualified at once – or with very little training – to enter Government service; there were men who were not only familiar with coastwise waters, tides, currents and other details essential to patrol duties, but yachtsmen who held the best sort of pilot's certificates..."

The seminal beginnings of the Star Class can be traced back to the East Coast, where William Gardner designed the smallest keel sloop of its day (1907). As the Star one-design evolved, it achieved enormous success as a racing class. It proved to be a performance boat "for men of ability but moderate means." The class gained recognition nationally, and then internationally, before becoming the largest one-design class in the world.

Among Joe Jessop's list of winnings in the Star Class are the 1924, 1926 and 1927 Pacific Coast Star Championships, the 1925 Star Internationals raced on Long Island Sound, and the 1928 Gold Star Series, to name but a few.

➤

1923

◆

The postwar year of 1923 showed signs of a rally for San Diego. Ed Peterson and Joe Jessop got together and built the first Star boat on the bay. Though the launching of *Windward* (sail #213) did not attract throngs of people, it was a momentous occasion. Joe Jessop's progress through the ranks of the National and International Star fleet would launch San Diego into an international yachting arena. Ironically, the events of those unsettling years set the club on its inevitable path toward victory.

Courtesy of San Diego Maritime Museum

Clem Stose entered his 56' yawl **Teva** in the 1926 Honolulu Race (which he won in 1928). This photo, from the San Diego Yacht Club's Private Collection, shows a group of illustrious sailors on board **Teva**. In the front row are: (unknown), Commodore Albert Soiland M.D., Clem Stose, Walter Trepte, Albert Frost, Richard Buell, Ash Bown (then only 14) and Captain Lew B. Harris (at 71 years of age). Standing on the cabin-top are Commodore Clarence W. MacFarlane, Gerard Nickerson, (unknown), and Alonzo de Jessop (farthest right).

Teva had a good chance of winning on handicap that year but she came up three hours and 35 minutes short on corrected time. She might have done considerably better if she hadn't lost all of her light air gear – her spinnaker pole, her ballooner and her jib topsail – before she encountered the light going at the end of the race!

Rich Goben is currently the captain of the vessels for Invader Cruises, which provide charters on San Diego Bay. Carolyn Johnson photographed Captain Goben in full regalia on board the 151' schooner **Invader**. Goben has honed his skills as a navigator/ skipper over his twenty-year career, while serving as captain on board many of California's most prestigious sailing ships. An interesting excursion from Goben's duties on board the more traditional sailing vessels occurred in 1979-80 when he got involved in San Diego's 12-Meter campaign. In 1982, Goben again entered the arena as the navigator on board all three practice boats. Once in Newport, Rhode Island for the 1983 Cup races, Rich served on the **Tamaqua**, gathering weather and course information throughout the races.

The winner of the 1926 Honolulu Race (which later became known as the Transpac) was the 151' steel schooner **Invader**. Built in 1905, the ship was designed by A.S. Cheseborough, nephew of the famous yacht designer, Nathanael Herreshoff. **Invader** raced in the Big Class of racing yachts, though she was not involved in racing for the America's Cup. The boat was sailed from the East Coast through the newly opened Panama Canal in 1919, and ended up in San Francisco. Once there, she sailed out of the San Francisco Yacht Club.

Capable of sailing up to 21 knots (24 mph) with a crew of 30, Invader set a 24-hour Transpac record during the 1926 Honolulu Race. She sailed 300 nautical miles, noon to noon, a record which stood until 1977 when **Merlin** finally surpassed it.

In 1983, Invader arrived in San Diego, where she has since operated daily as a charter vessel. With her years as a fast racing vessel behind her, she still offers a glimpse of her grand sailing heritage.

Bette McHenry

1927

◆

The year 1927 saw the rise of another yacht club in San Diego. Initially discovered by Sebastián Viscaíno, Mission Bay was called False Bay for many years. The shallow waters of Mission Bay were impassable for large ships, but offered an almost idyllic setting for small boat sailing.

In order to envision what Mission Bay might have looked like in the 1920's, one would have to hark back to the Derby Dyke. In order to keep San Diego Harbor navigable, the San Diego River had been diverted from San Diego Harbor by means of the Derby Dyke. (The Derby Dyke was later replaced by a more efficient levee system.)

Courtesy of San Diego Historical Society, Ticor Collection

San Diego Harbor was saved, but Mission Bay was left to the mercy of natural forces. Until the Mission Bay jetties were

In 1903, Mission Bay offered a place to row or sail a shallow draft boat, and (best of all) a place to cool off during the hot summer months.

Courtesy of
San Diego Historical Society,
Photograph Collection

Courtesy of San Diego Historical Society, Ticor Collection

completed in the early 1950's, and plans laid out for the development of an aquatic park, Mission Bay was a series of mud flats and marsh lands interrupted by a few narrow winding channels.

This early 1900's photo, with Mission Bay in the background, overlooks the farming area of Pacific Beach! With no connecting bridges at that time, San Diego was a fair distance from Mission Bay and the beach area.

For a handful of sailing enthusiasts Mission Bay offered enough water for shallow draft boats such as the *Skimmer* and *Flapper* class. The first Club members, headed by Tom Scripps (of the prominent Scripps family) seemed to share a certain delight in the unassuming nature of the young Club. The original aim of the Mission Bay Yacht Club was to have:

"A Corinthian Yacht Club where, regardless of one's station in life, we meet on a common ground - our favorite pastime, yachting."

Articles in the 1927 *San Diego Union* generated a good deal of excitement in anticipation of the arrival of the bark *Star of India*. The enthusiastic reporter who kept the *Star of India* in the headlines, well past her historic arrival, was the *Union's* waterfront reporter Gerald F. MacMullen.

"Jerry" MacMullen's "waterfront" career spanned more than fifty years of his productive life (1897-1981). An entire book on his life could only do him justice, for he was a man of extraordinary talent. He was a journalist by profession, a historian by predisposition, a sailor of notable ability, a natural-born storyteller and an artist of considerable talent.

MacMullen's contributions to various local historical societies were reputedly so vast that you would be hard pressed to find a club or society he had not been a member of at one time or other.

Among MacMullen's long list of associations, he completed the San Diego Yacht Club's first history (in 1926), while acting as Staff Commodore. He was also the owner of *Butcher Boy* during that period, and sailed her to many first place finishes.

Courtesy of Mission Bay Yacht Club

Tom Scripps was elected to serve as the Mission Bay Yacht Club's first Commodore in 1927. The first clubhouse was located on Crown Point; it later re-located to El Carmel Point. From the Club's inception, it has held true to its ideal. The MBYC is still very much a "family" club, where people of modest means can enjoy the many levels of small boat sailing in a lovely environment.

This 1949 photo from the Fiesta Bahia Regatta captures three top sailors, all of whom would go on to leave their own mark on San Diego's sailing history. Humorously captioned the "Goon Squad" of 1949, from left to right stand, Carl Eichenlaub Jr., Bob Gales and Leroy Lenhart, who received trophies for the Skimmer Class.

Courtesy of Mission Bay Yacht Club

The Mission Bay Yacht Club has hosted many national and international yachting competitions. The first Lightning Fleet to be chartered in California was formed through the MBYC in the late 1940's.

Courtesy of Mission Bay Yacht Club

*Today, the Mission Bay Yacht Club is at the hub of small boat sailing.
It continues to bring up through the ranks national and international sailing
champions. Five-time World Snipe Champion Earl Elms, Jeff Lenhart (winner of
many Snipe titles), Craig Leweck and Eric Krebs lead the list of top sailors,
which continues to grow.*

*Mission Bay will play an important role in the 1992 America's Cup races by
providing land-based facilities for visiting foreign syndicates.*

Courtesy of San Diego Maritime Museum

In 1927, the bark Star of India was towed into San Diego Bay. On board were Jerry MacMullen and other members of the crew.

Courtesy of San Diego Historical Society, Photograph Collection

Poised on the deck of the Star of India, Jerry MacMullen reflected on the sailing ship he was so instrumental in bringing to San Diego.

The Star has a long and impressive sailing history, which the Maritime Museum has kept well-preserved. Not only has the world's oldest merchant sailing ship been fully restored, the Maritime Museum has supported every endeavor to recapture her valiant career. A collection of diaries, letters and logs of the Star, dating from the time she was engaged as a British emigrant ship, has been compiled and edited by Craig Arnold (current librarian at the museum), and published under the title Euterpe. As an emigrant ship, she made 21 west to east round-the-world voyages, carrying at times over 400 emigrants per voyage. Euterpe was the original name of the iron-hulled ship, which was built in Ramsey, Isle of Man, in 1863.

Courtesy of Port of San Diego

Among Jerry MacMullen's myriad talents, he applied his artistic vision to both painting and photography. This 1936 photograph taken on board the Pacific Queen by Jerry MacMullen, courtesy of the Port of San Diego Photo Archives, is just one of an enormous collection of his photos.

On very special occasions the Star of India sets sail once again. The commands, not often heard on a modern ship, are passed along by the wind:

"Raise tacks and sheets! says the Captain...
Main topsail haul!
Let go and haul! says the Captain...
The mate, on the forecastle, looks out for the head yards.
Let go and haul! Topgallant yard's well..."

Courtesy of Dale Frost, Port of San Diego

Dale Frost, Port of San Diego

Dale Frost, Port of San Diego

A large crew is required in order to man each station on the sailing ship. The volunteer crew for the Star train year-round in anticipation of her historic voyages.

One of the most exhilarating jobs on board sends the sailor aloft to work with the huge sails from the yards. Sailing literature does not belie the potential danger in this job. Many a sailor was lost, after being pitched from the yards as the ship rolled in a furious sea.

Bob Covarrubias

Aye! There is mighty work to be done on board, requiring strength and stamina.

The singing of sea chanties often accompanied backbreaking jobs such as hauling away on the anchor.

Bob Covarrubias

Attention to detail is what keeps the Maritime Museum's ships in top form. Pictured is Walt Jacobsen, the ship's carver, who was instrumental in restoring the Star's Euterpe figurehead in 1987.

Bob Covarrubias

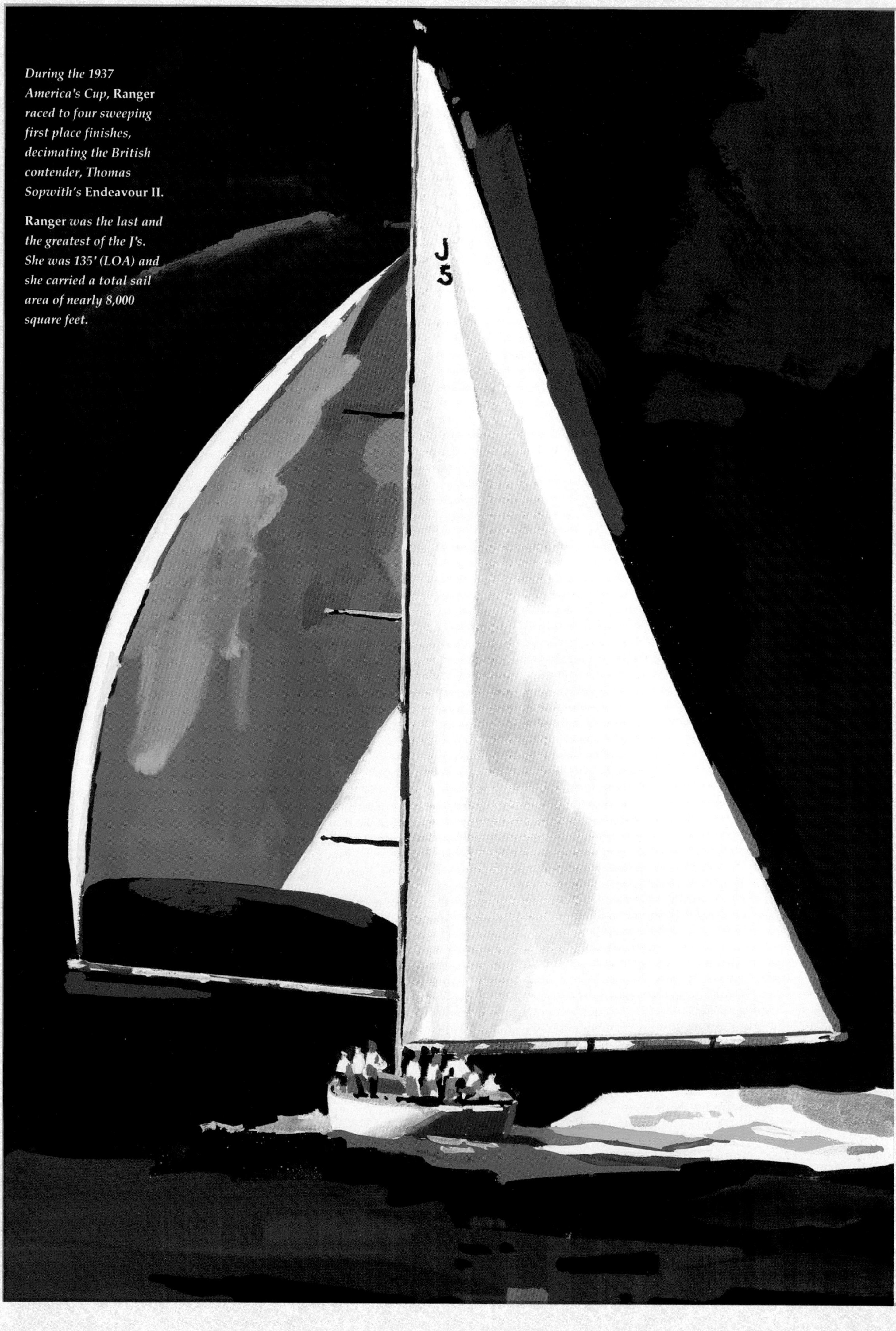

During the 1937
America's Cup, **Ranger**
raced to four sweeping
first place finishes,
decimating the British
contender, Thomas
Sopwith's **Endeavour II**.

Ranger *was the last and
the greatest of the J's.
She was 135' (LOA) and
she carried a total sail
area of nearly 8,000
square feet.*

Chapter Six

On the Wind's Highway

1930's

◆

I t was quite surprising, considering the Stock Market Crash of 1929, that there was any sailing at all in San Diego during the years preceding World War II. They were hard times indeed, but the sailors kept sailing, through good times and bad, on whatever boats they could muster. When the coffers were empty, the yachts got smaller; when economies stabilized new designs prospered.

One such new design was the PC-class, which owes its origin to Joe Jessop Sr. and designer/builder George Kettenburg Jr. (of Kettenburg Marine). The two young men approached George's father with the idea of his financing the project. George Kettenburg Sr., who had already recognized his son's natural talent for boatbuilding, gave his approval and the PC got underway in 1929.

The PCs were an instant success, with 35 boats built before World War II, and 48 boats built in the post-war years.

A favorite Yacht Club story, which still lingers in the rafters, recounts one rainy San Diego afternoon in 1930, when the PC sailors came up with the idea of racing the Herreshoff S-class in Hawaii. The dimensions of the boats were similar, and the competition would be stiff. A sole handicap to the whole idea was how to transport the boats to Hawaii. Since yachtsmen's efforts throughout World War I had been so lauded by the Navy, Joe Jessop decided to ask the Navy to transport four PCs to Hawaii for the series. The story has it that the Navy was more than receptive of the idea, offering to carry the fleet on a naval transport vessel. The eleven day voyage went by quickly, with Navy sailors side-by-side with the local yachtsmen, as they prepared their boats for the races. Mr. Jessop reported that the San Diego

Courtesy of San Diego Historical Society, Ticor Collection

▲
PC sailing on San Diego waters dates back to the early 1930's, when Joe Jessop and George Kettenburg Jr. decided to build a 32' daysailer suitable for San Diego waters.

Paul Kettenburg glides by the classic PC Wings (#8), confident in the windward ability of his boat.

The Kettenburg PCs marked the beginning of a series of successful Kettenburg designs. George Kettenburg Jr. was considered a natural-born naval architect, even though he never formally studied the subject. He began building boats in his father's backyard on Point Loma during his early teens. His father's keen business sense would later guide him through the rigors of the marine business. George Jr.'s younger brother, Paul, joined the family firm in 1943.

The backyard operation expanded, and by 1929 the Kettenburg Boat & Engine Company moved to the foot of Dickens Street and became Kettenburg Boatworks. By 1956, the business had incorporated under the name of Kettenburg Marine.

Courtesy of Paul Kettenburg

Courtesy of San Diego Maritime Museum

The PC-class was active throughout the war years. PCs gradually replaced the R-class boats and began to race in other locations. The PCs were often trailered up to Newport Beach, where a series of weekend team sailing events became popular. After World War II, the popularity of the class spread along the West Coast, from Seattle to San Francisco and Los Angeles.

PCs narrowly edged out the Herreshoff S-boats after six weeks of racing.

When the races were over and victory assured, the boats were sold in Hawaii, and the sailors prepared for their journey home. Then came the question: "How are we going to get home?" The Navy came to the rescue once again, as the new battle cruiser *Chicago* returned to port in Honolulu from sea-trials. *Chicago's* next mission was to attempt to make the fastest Hawaii-to-San Francisco passage in naval history.

The twelve young sailors, fresh from their own victory, were then offered berths in the Admiral's quarters, as there was no Admiral on board for the passage! Joe Jessop was relegated to the task of "civilian observer" and he did, in fact, observe the fastest Hawaii-to-San Francisco passage of that time.

Two other yacht clubs struggled through the pre-war years while trying to get established. They were the Coronado Yacht Club (orginally housed in the Hotel Del's Boat-house) and the Southwestern Yacht Club (currently located in La Playa on Point Loma). However, World War II was in the offing and the yachtsmen and their boats would be called back into service.

The Kettenburg family arrived in San Diego in 1910, and completed building their first home on Kellogg Street in 1913. Their chimney, rising three levels, identifies the Kettenburgs' residence near the center of the photo. Paul Kettenburg recalls the very early days of Kettenburg Marine, when young George (at age 15) built the family's first boat in their backyard.

In the distance, looking east, the Roseville Star & Crescent ferry landing at La Playa can be seen, stretching out from the Pavilion dance hall building. This is the current location of the San Diego Yacht Club.

Courtesy of
San Diego Historical Society,
Ticor Collection

Courtesy of San Diego Historical Society, Photograph Collection

Neva Sullaway

The thriving fishing industry would feel the effects of the war years as well, as the big tuna boats were taken up for war service, painted gray and armed with depth charges and machine guns.

After the bombing of Pearl Harbor on December 7, 1941, San Diego Harbor's entrance was completely netted (only naval vessels and necessary supply ships were allowed to pass) and sailing was limited to the bay waters. Civilians were enlisted to man aircraft spotting stations and coast and harbor watches.

The 11 1/2' Penguin dinghy became a popular boat in this era. It was a small, economical boat capable of close-quarter maneuvering. Kettenburg Marine responded to popular demand by turning out eighteen of the plywood dinghies in 1942.

While sailing was growing in accordance with the times in San Diego, the East Coast continued to produce handsome yachts for both racing and cruising, many of which proudly sail on San Diego waters today.

Originally built in 1930 at the Dauntless Shipyard in Connecticut, the John Alden-designed staysail schooner *Dauntless* is a sight to behold on San Diego Bay. The 71' (LOA) schooner was named after the shipyard, which in turn was named after the 1870 America's Cup schooner *Dauntless*.

Dauntless was sailed down from San Francisco in 1984 by her current owner, Paul Plotts. Plotts has stayed in contact with the schooner's original owner, Horace B. Merwin, and it was through Mr. Merwin that Plott's was able to chart *Dauntless*'s outstanding sailing career.

Alden schooners have always carried with them the distinction of being well-built, comfortable at sea, and capable of

Almost any modern day view of the harbor leaves a strong impression of a once thriving local industry. The fishing industry has gone through many transitions. The old technique of bait boat and pole fishing was prominent from the 1930's to the 1950's. Then San Diego fishermen developed the innovative purse seine method of fishing (in the 1960's) utilizing huge nets, enabling the boats to pull in larger catches. The 1970's and 1980's saw the passage of environmental acts, which greatly impacted the local tuna industry. Now many of the large purse seiners head off to foreign waters, leaving San Diego to the past.

The Tunaman's Memorial on Shelter Island reads:

"Honoring those that built an industry and remembering those that departed this harbor in the sun and did not return."

This photo taken at 1:55 p.m. on April 10, 1943 certainly describes wartime San Diego. The busy street scene is at Fourth and Broadway.

making swift passages. *Dauntless* is a fine example of the schooner of that era.

Only six days after *Dauntless* was christened, she set sail in the 1930 Bermuda Race. The 650-mile East Coast race from New London, Connecticut to Bermuda was the premiere event of the sailing season, attracting up to 30 boats. The object of the Bermuda Race was to encourage the designing, building and sailing of seaworthy yachts for ocean racing. Held every other

Courtesy of San Diego Historical Society, Ticor Collection

year, the Bermuda Race became the gauge for measuring the performance of the newest and fastest boats on the water.

Racing against a fleet of seasoned yachts, *Dauntless* swept the fleet to a first-place finish. This would be the first in a long list of wins for *Dauntless*, a list which is still being added to today.

Headlines in the Oct 7, 1990 *San Diego Union* sports page announced:

"*DAUNTLESS* TAKES TOP HONORS"

The article about the San Diego to Ensenada Yacht Race read:

"Paul Plotts' 61-foot [LWL-length waterline] schooner, *Dauntless*, from the host Club [Southwestern Yacht Club] won the overall Performance Handicap Racing Fleet title in the 62 1/2-mile race."

Dauntless outdistances her longtime rival the 86' (LOA-length overall) schooner Astor (built in 1924). Dauntless is easily recognizable by her graceful lines and the American flag flown off the leech of her mainsail.

Bob Covarrubias

Dale Frost

Paul Plotts initiated and each year hosts the Annual Billy Bones Schooner Race from Mission Bay to San Diego. A highlight of the event is the raft-up in Mission Bay, where Paul's Billy Bones Tavern (located in Pacific Beach) supplies the "all you can eat and drink" afternoon.

The start of the 1990 Billy Bones Race off the Mission Bay Jetty featured the classic schooners Dauntless, Maid of Kent, Golden Eagle and Albatross.

Owner/Skipper Paul Plotts is at the wheel of Dauntless, obviously enjoying an afternoon on the bay. Dauntless can be seen sailing on the bay on almost any Sunday afternoon.

Paul recounted the story he had heard after the race about the International Ocean Racing boat trailing the stern of *Dauntless* for some hours during the race. One weary crewmember onboard the I.O.R. racer finally broke down in frustration and asked gruffly,

"Who the hell are those two boats we can't catch?"

After a few moments of all eyes squinting at the horizon, the disbelieving skipper realized the incongruity, there were not two boats ahead of them but only one – the sixty-year veteran schooner *Dauntless*.

Another local yacht which hails from the 1930's is Keith and Vikki Korporaal's 56' yawl *Orion*. A classic beauty, *Orion* was first christened *Edlu* when she was owned by Rudolf Schaefer of Schaefer Breweries. Designed by Olin Stephens and custom-built by Nevin's Shipyard in City Island, New York (1934), she was immediately put through her paces as a starter in the 1934 Bermuda Race.

Twenty-nine boats came to the starting line that year. Among them were such proven racers as *Dauntless*, Olin Stephen's *Dorade, Stormy Weather, Flying Cloud* and *Teragram*.

Dauntless is in a class all her own.

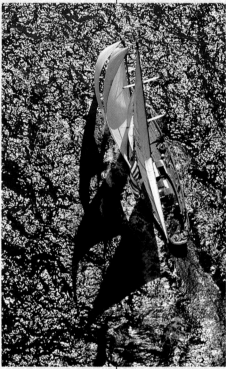

Dale Frost

Dale Frost, Port of San Diego

The fleet apparently had to contend with some high winds that year. A 1934 account of the race, as reported in *Rudder* magazine, gives a good deal of the credit to *Edlu's* helmsman Bob Bavier for driving her "for all she was worth" through the high winds. The winds kicked up quite a swell and some yachts did not fare as well as *Edlu:*

"One well-known schooner, one of the best in the race, reported all hands were sick, so sick in fact that they took sail off and let her coast, losing all interest in the race, and probably everything else."

Edlu, now *Orion*, was the first sloop ever to win the ocean race to Bermuda. After proving herself the best ocean racer of 1934, *Edlu (Orion)* went on to further lengthen her list of winnings.

Dale Frost

Crews of the Ancient Mariner Class (yachts of traditional design and construction) are typically adept at all phases of sailing and racing, especially in the "serious fun" category. Notice their ability to hang on, laugh and balance a glass while under sail!

Pictured are sailors Trudy Wood (farthest forward), Linda Hovland (middle) and John Frost (aft on the bowsprit).

The 1990 Fourth Annual America's Schooner Cup Race, hosted by the Kona Kai International Yacht Club, brought fifteen West Coast schooners to the starting line.

The 1987 ASC winner, Dauntless, is moments away from passing Rose of Sharon, a racing companion since the 1930 Bermuda Race!

Neva Sullaway

Rosenfeld Collection, Mystic Seaport Museum

Edlu's original sloop design was later altered to a yawl rig. Her young designer, Olin Stephens, was fast making a name for himself with his 6-Meter designs and ocean racers, such as Dorade. The December 1930 issue of Yachting magazine had a portrait of Olin on the Hall of Fame page with a caption that began:

"To have achieved a reputation as a clever helmsman, successful racing skipper, and at the same time to have earned a name as a naval architect with many fast yachts to one's credit is something that does not often fall to the lot of anyone at the age of 20...."

Dale Frost

Orion sails on San Diego waters for pleasure. The Korporaals still race her, and Orion is available for private charters.

She is maintained in Bristol condition and the craftsmanship in her interior is something to be seen. Utilizing exotic woods such as koa and ebony, Orion recalls the elegant days of sailing.

Dale Frost

America's Cup History

1930-1958

Not surprisingly, Harold Vanderbilt approached Olin Stephens in 1936 to help design an America's Cup boat. Vanderbilt had already successfully defended the America's Cup twice, once in 1930 and again in 1934 in J-class boats designed by Starling Burgess. Also equally unsurprising was that Olin and his brother Rod Stephens would join in a design team with Starling Burgess, to help produce the magnificent racing yacht *Ranger*. In light of the design approaches of the 1990's, it is interesting to note that the testing of scale models in ship model basins began with *Ranger*.

By World War II, it seemed that another grand chapter in America's Cup history was about to close. The design excesses of the Big Class and the exciting innovations from the J- Class had had their day. Nat Herreshoff was no longer designing America's Cup boats and Sir Thomas Lipton had long since left his quest for the Cup to others. It was an era that had not quite turned the corner to a new one, and so it lingered in its grandness. There would be a long and silent pause in Cup racing until 1958.

The graceful lines of Ranger undoubtedly belonged to the J-class, which originated when the Universal Rule came into being in 1901. The J-Class, of which only two (Shamrock V and Endeavour) survive on the water today, tended to have a waterline length from between 80 to 87 feet, with an overall length of 120 to 135 feet.

➤

Image acquired in honor of Franz Schneider, Rosenfeld Collection, Mystic Seaport Museum

▲

Harold Vanderbilt is at the wheel, in a rare moment of relaxation during the 1937 America's Cup series. Olin Stephens is standing to his right, looking rather contemplative. Rod Stephens is perched on a winch playing his accordian.

Image acquired in honor of Franz Schneider, Rosenfeld Collection, Mystic Seaport Museum

San Diego sailors have been in the forefront of national and international Star Class racing for three-quarters of a century.

Chapter Seven

Of Fine Sailors and Fast Yachts

1945

◆

When the Navy removed the netting at the harbor's entrance in 1945, it signalled the beginning of a new era in yachting, not only for San Diego but for the whole nation.

Among the sailing events that survived during the war years, the Star Class found San Diego sailors at the forefront of international competition. The 1937 International Star Champion, Milt Wegeforth (son of Dr. Harold Wegeforth, founder of the world-famous San Diego Zoo), sailed for the San Diego Yacht Club.

dewitt '91

The 1944 Star Internationals, sailed on Lake Michigan, brought to the starting line two sailors destined to leave their mark on San Diego's sailing history: Gerald Driscoll and Malin Burnham. With Driscoll as skipper and Burnham as crew, the sailors formed a winning combination. Both Driscoll (who was to open Driscoll's Boatyard in 1947) and Burnham would go on to play an important role in local sailing, not only as top sailors in their own right, but as central figures in San Diego's twenty-seven year involvement in America's Cup racing.

Courtesy of Malin Burnham

Tracing Malin Burnham's sailing career is like holding a kaleidoscope up to the sun; rotating it slightly, the mix of colors falls into luminous patterns. Among all the colorful patterns you will find a shrewd businessman, a sailing champion, and one of the key players in several of the America's Cup campaigns. First, however, you should look straight to the man: the epitome of the natural sailor, an entrepreneur cast in the mold of his grandfather John Burnham, and the consummate visionary, willing to take the ultimate risks for victory.

Burnham came early to the game of sailing. He was racing Starlets by the age of 10, and by 15 he had acquired his first Star boat. Within two years, he would be on his way to the 1946 Star World Championships in Stamford, Connecticut, as skipper. Burnham asked Lowell North (then 15 years old) to crew for him. History was already in the making. The boys would not only come home champions, but they were also the youngest competitors ever to win the Star Worlds. For both sailors, it was only the beginning of a long and successful sailing career.

Among the sailing fraternity, Lowell North is known as the "Pope." This eminent quality was awarded to Lowell as part of a saying about Paul Elvstrom. Elvstrom, a Danish sailor and boatbuilder, won four Olympic Gold Medals, more than a dozen world championships in various one-design classes, and was considered the god of sailing! Local

Courtesy of Malin Burnham

Standing in the winner's circle at the age of 17 might have seemed like a climactic moment in Malin Burnham's career, yet Burnham would continue to race in the Star Class for another highly-competitive thirty years.

Courtesy of Malin Burnham

sailors who knew North struggled to find a place for him in the hierarchy, so they said:

"If Elvstrom is God, than Lowell North must be the Pope!"

The impressive sailing history of Lowell North spans nearly fifty years. It begins with the job transfer of his father, a geophysicist, to San Diego. In an effort to placate his son after a decade of moving to different jobs around the country, Willard North bought a Star for his son and himself to race. Lowell recalled their first season of racing in the San Diego Star fleet:

"We started last and we finished last!"

The experience did not seem to dissuade the young sailor, as he gradually took over the job of skippering the boat. His first real break into the sailing world came when Malin Burnham asked the 15-year-old to crew for him in the 1946 Star Worlds.

Curiously enough, the young sailor did not bound right into the world of sailmaking. In fact, North did not find his niche until the age of 28, when the aircraft engineer moved into a job as a stress analyst, testing fiberglass tail sections. While working for a local La Mesa firm, North began producing a line of sail battens. This small side venture did not pan out particularly well, as the battens proved to be too abrasive and cut the sails. It did, however, draw his attention to the sails themselves with their aerodynamic design and resultant air foil shape.

Courtesy of
San Diego Historical Society,
Union Tribune Collection

The year 1957 proved to be a pivotal one for North. He won his first Star Worlds in Havana, Cuba. Soon after, North opened his first sail loft in an upstairs room in a building at the B Street Pier. North was hoping to build faster, more competitive sails. He admits that his small company was not an overnight success story. It would take a few years before

Courtesy of San Diego Historical Society, Union Tribune Collection

Courtesy of
San Diego Historical Society,
Union Tribune Collection

they got a consistent line up and running. Those first sails belonged to the Snipe and Star classes.

Success came quickly. North won the 1959 and 1960 Star World Championships back-to-back. Though it would be another 13 years before North won his record-breaking fourth Star Worlds, his name was already etched in silver and destined to be golden.

North credits the enormous surge forward in his own sailmaking business to the introduction of dacron cloth, replacing the much less efficient cotton sails. His father helped him build his new loft at Anchorage Lane on Shelter Island. From there, North Sails would grow, not only nationally but internationally, as would North's own stature among the all-time sailing greats.

In 1964, North won a bronze medal in the Dragon Class, and, in 1968, he and his crew Peter Barrett (1964 Finn Silver medalist) proudly brought home an Olympic Gold Medal to San Diego. North was elected to the San Diego Sports Hall of Fame in 1969 and was named Yachtsman of the Year for the third time by the San Diego Association of Yacht Clubs!

Among all the accolades derived from his business and sailing successes, North never missed an opportunity to stress how important his crew was, or his co-workers at the North loft:

"I guess if I wanted to leave my kids [Danny, Holly and Julie] with one thing, it would be perspective. The best part is people...we're all in this together."

The above sounds like the end of a nice story, but it's barely the beginning. The "Pope" was just starting his reign.

▼

The 1990's still find Lowell North most at home on his own boat. North spends much of his time cruising the waters most sailors only dream about.

Bob Covarrubias

▲

North, with crewmember Peter Barrett, won his historic fourth Star Worlds in 1973. Among North's ingredients for sailing success was his obsessional attention to detail and preparation before the race. It has been said of him that he won many races before he ever got to the starting line!

In 1973, the starting line was packed with the world's best sailors. Thirteen countries were represented in the 56 boat fleet racing in San Diego. Six Gold Star World champions competed.

North would go on to win his fourth Star Worlds in 1973, and then shift his focus to ocean racing. A whole new list of victories would describe his ocean racing career: the Quarter-Ton Worlds, the One-Ton North Americans and Worlds, the SORC series, on up to his involvement with the 12-Meter trials of 1967 and 1977.

From one great sailor to another, perhaps Dennis Conner said it best in his book *No Excuse To Lose*:

"I think that now [circa 1978] Lowell must be the best all-round sailor in the world."

1946

◆

There were equally exciting developments on the local sailing scene in the latter part of the 1940's and early 1950's.

George Kettenburg Jr. had a yacht design all laid out and ready for production as World War II drew to a close. The 46' PCC would hit the water by 1946 and begin a whole new series of popular Kettenburg boats.

► *The 46' PCC (Pacific Cruising Class) was modelled on the ideal racer/cruiser design concepts of the time. The class quickly developed along the West Coast, helping to bring some silver back to San Diego. In 1946, Milt Wegeforth won the Lipton Cup sailing his PCC Ray. It had been fifteen years since the Cup had been in the S.D.Y.C.'s trophy case.*

Courtesy of Paul Kettenburg

Courtesy of Paul Kettenburg

Courtesy of Paul Kettenburg

1947

◆

While West Coast designers/builders pursued the ideal boat for Pacific waters, East Coast firms continued to build yachts to their own specifications. By the late 1940's, Olin Stephens, as part of Sparkman & Stephens, Inc., had reached worldwide prominence as a yacht designer. It seemed that even when he was asked to design a cruiser, he could not resist giving her the lines of a racer.

A beautiful example of a Stephen's design during this period is represented by the San Diego yawl *Pacifica*, a most inspiring sight on the bay. Currently owned by Jack and Ann Frost of the San Diego Yacht Club, the 49' yawl was designed by Olin Stephens and custom-built at Nevin's Shipyard, New York, in 1947. Her first owner was the prominent Mr. Fuller of Fuller Brush Co.

An interesting aspect of *Pacifica's* design (which was later added by Fuller against the advice of Stephens) was her extruded aluminum mast. *Pacifica* was the first yacht built for offshore cruising with this innovation. It worked well on the yawl, and during the 1950's and 1960's, *Pacifica* would begin to amass an impressive offshore racing record.

One of *Pacifica's* owners, well known to the scientific world as a nuclear physicist, was the Italian Gabriel Giannini. It was Giannini who sailed *Pacifica* over to the Mediterranean and later sailed her back through the Panama Canal, bringing *Pacifica* to her final home port of San Diego.

Rosenfeld Collection,
Mystic Seaport Museum

This photo of Pacifica (formerly called Eroica) was traced back to the Rosenfeld Collection, Mystic Seaport Museum. It places her sailing along the Eastern seaboard in grand style. Although she was first built for cruising, her sleek lines placed Pacifica in the forefront of offshore racing. In 1960, she was first to finish in the Miami to Nassau race; in 1963, she was first in her class in the prestigious S.O.R.C. series, and the last split-rigged (two-masted) yacht to claim that distinction.

Pacifica has not only maintained her stately appearance over her fifty-year career, but the cruising yawl also continues to outpace the racers in her class. She was first to finish in the 1978 Ancient Mariner San Diego to Maui race, which she sailed in 13 days and 12 hours. Pacifica also continues to capture local titles such as the 1986 Yesteryear Regatta.

Dale Frost

1951

◆

West Coast ocean races such as the Transpac (formerly the Honolulu Race) offered some amazing moments in San Diego's sailing history in the 1950's.

The 1951 race will be forever etched in the annals of Transpac history for the miraculous man-overboard rescue which took place that year. On board one of the leading boats, *L'Apache,* was 40-year-old Ted Sierks. On July 11th, seven days out of San Pedro harbor and still 840 miles from Honolulu, Sierks was knocked overboard while trying to repair the preventer tackle on the boom. At the time, the 73' cutter was carrying both a spinnaker and a staysail set inside the spinnaker in a 20 knot breeze. The boat was sailing at top speed when the "Man Overboard" call was heard. Sierks just managed to catch the end of the taffrail log; its spinning blades cut his wrist and fingers before breaking his only lifeline to the boat. By the time the crew had doused the sails and returned to the area, Sierks was already lost in mountainous seas.

The emergency call kept six racing yachts scanning the area for any sign of Sierks. Then four Destroyers, three Destroyer escorts and a SB-17 arrived to sweep the area. As Sierks described it, his chance for survival was about "one in a

A local San Diego resident, William F. Sullaway (Navy Lieutenant and Engineering Officer) was on board the Navy Destroyer Escort Munro to capture the moment. This photo, accompanying Sierk's story, appeared in the September 1951 issue of Life magazine.

million." Several times throughout the long night, Sierks could make out the lights of the search vessels passing close by, but they were not close enough to pick out the small beam of light from his life ring. The morning brought renewed hope, yet with each passing ship, Sierks realized his infinitesimal being amidst the enormity of the Pacific Ocean.

The rescue effort was called off, but Captain John Lindbeck, on board the Destroyer Escort *Munro*, decided to take one last sweep of the area. Sierks was miraculously spotted and pulled on board the *Munro* some thirty hours after having fallen overboard!

After the astonishing search and rescue, the *Munro* limped into Honolulu Harbor on one boiler, without enough fuel to get to nearby Pearl Harbor.

This amazing open-ocean photograph, taken from the air by a reporter from one of the Honolulu newspapers, shows Novia Del Mar steaming along under full sail. The photo was made available by Paul Kettenburg, who crewed on Novia Del Mar in the 1955 Transpac. His experiences on board attest to the windy conditions that year. Novia Del Mar blew out two spinnakers in one day in 50-mile-an-hour rain squalls.

Novia Del Mar was perhaps one of the most celebrated yachts in San Diego during her eighteen-year reign on the ocean racing circuit.

Courtesy of San Diego Maritime Museum

The local San Diego entry Evening Star, owned by the Trepte family, was involved in the search for eight hours, yet still managed to finish the race fifth overall.

The 1955 Transpac was memorable for several reasons. Those who sailed in the race, remember extraordinarily high winds, which pushed the forerunners along to new record passages. Morning Star crossed the finish line to set a new record of 9:15:05:10.

The third boat to cross the finish line that year was Novia Del Mar, owned by John P. Scripps of the San Diego Yacht Club. The 89' LOA Alden ketch would show her mettle in her first Transpac, and go on to represent San Diego proudly in many ocean races.

Courtesy of Paul Kettenberg

America's Cup History

1958

In contrast to the expansion of the racer/cruiser divisions was the rise in popularity of the Meter Classes, which tended to be pure racing thoroughbreds.

The development of the 6-, 8-, 9-, 10- and 12-Meter classes can be traced back to 1907, when thirteen nations assembled to design an International Rule, which would bring order to the chaos of racing yacht measurement. (American interest in the Meter boats developed only after a rule modification in 1919.)

The first large influx of Meter boats began in 1927, when a syndicate of Long Island yachtsmen ordered 14 identical 10-Meters from Starling Burgess's design to be built in Germany by Aberking and Rasmussen. Unlike the smaller 6-Meters, the 10-Meters were 60' in length overall. (The number designation of the Meter boats does not refer to their length, but represents a complex equation which takes into account length overall (LOA) and waterline (LWL) length, measured girth, draft, sail area, etc.)

As a way of skirting the U.S. duty on the importation of foreign boats, they were shipped to Halifax, Nova Scotia, and then sailed down "on their bottoms" to Long Island Sound. After enduring the harsh conditions of the North Atlantic, the 10-Meters soon gained a reputation for being fast boats to windward, and though inclined "to sail on their ear" in a strong breeze, they proved seaworthy. The new fleet certainly caught the eye of one local New York yacht designer, Olin Stephens.

Courtesy of C.F. Koehler

Currently owned by 26-year-old C.F. Koehler of Koehler Kraft on Shelter Island, the 10-Meter Sally dates back to that first voyage of 10-Meters into U.S. waters in 1927. Her hull number is 12 and she still races today on San Diego Bay against her sister-ship Branta (hull #7), as well as other Ancient Mariners.

Once owned by another well-known local yachtsman, Walter Trepte, Sally raced under the San Diego Yacht Club colors in the 1940's.

C.F. Koehler sailed Sally down to San Diego from Santa Cruz in 1986. He has spent the last four years involved in her "sailing restoration." In between sailing and racing Sally, C.F. has restored her wooden hull, interior, rigging and her teak deck.

When one asks C.F. why he spends so much time, money and elbow grease on the classic yacht, he is quick to answer:

"There is nothing in my life that has given me, and the people who sail on Sally, so much pleasure."

Neva Sullaway

Neva Sullaway

The 12-Meters had gained acceptance as a racing class in the U.S. as early as the 1920's. When they first appeared at Larchmont, New York, they were considered "small" in comparison to the massive rigged J-Boats and the larger schooners that dwarfed them. However, they were appealing simply because their smaller size represented a more reasonable financial investment. With some variation, the 12's were about 65' long and carried a crew of eleven.

▼ *Mitena was one of the early 12-Meters designed by L. Francis Herreshoff, and built in the U.S. in 1935. Her canoe-shaped stern, a Herreshoff trademark, made her recognizable amongst all the 12's at that time. Mitena, however, did not prove to be a winner for her owner, William Strawbridge (syndicate head for Intrepid in 1967).*

Rosenfeld Collection, Mystic Seaport Museum

Rosenfeld Collection, Mystic Seaport Museum

◄ *The 12-Meters ushered in a new era of America's Cup racing. There had been no Cup races held after Harold Vanderbilt's win on Ranger (in 1937) until 1958. Through the 1930's, 1940's and early 1950's the stage was being set for the next contest for the Auld Mug.*

San Diego continues
to be an active
maritime center with
an ever-changing
city skyline.

Chapter Eight

A Winning Boat is Priceless

1960's

◆

The last century has witnessed amazing changes along San Diego's waterfront. Gone are the days of sailing ships carrying their cargoes into port, docking at the long outstretching arms of the various wharves that dotted the inner harbor. There are no more cobblestones to be taken from Ballast Point, no more poems written about Whaler's Bight, nor any remnants of Dana's hide houses. Today, the shoreline curves around the bay, offering a completely different view from those early days. While much has been lost, much has been gained.

As San Diego surged forward in the 1960's and '70's, the buoyant atmosphere carried over into the yachting arena. A wave of top class sailors, designers and builders slowly gathered momentum, and would carry San Diego to the very crest of yachting achievement.

There was one sailor who was neither an Olympic Champion nor an America's Cup skipper, yet his name resurfaces throughout fifty years of San Diego's sailing history. Ash Bown was the 14-year-old cabin boy on Clem Stose's schooner *Teva*. Years later, he would take a badgering young sailor, Dennis Conner, ocean racing, just as Stose had taken him. Ash Bown dominated the local sailing scene for many years, on various types of yachts.

As a 14-year-old racing on board the 56' schooner to Hawaii in 1926, Bown wrote to his parents:

"...It sure was a lot of fun, for by that time the wind was

▼

The greatest strides forward for the harbor were made after 1962, when the San Diego Unified Port District was created. The Port District would oversee such major projects as the development of the public tidelands around San Diego Bay, while trying to shape the best possible future for the harbor and the growing city.

The Port District encompasses the cities of San Diego, National City, Chula Vista, Imperial Beach and Coronado.

▲

Turn-of-the-century San Diego offered quite a different perspective from the 1990's vistas.

Harbor Island expanded San Diego's docking facilities, and made available a long stretch of beautiful parkland called Spanish Landing for all to enjoy.

Bob Covarrubias

Bob Covarrubias

strong. We took all sails down except two and sailed her as a sloop. Every wave broke on the top and we were taking water in the cockpit....I liked it rough so I had a wonderful time all day, but everyone else was having a rotten time [because of seasickness]."

Bown was definitely a sailor in the making! Through the '50's and '60's, Ash Bown went on to win just about every type of Southern California ocean race. Among his victories were two Acapulco Races, a number of Ocean Racing division wins in the Newport-Ensenada Race, two San Diego Lipton Cup Challenges and five area O.R. championships.

Young Dennis Conner was certainly impressed by the sailing hero. After years of pestering Bown, Conner finally got invited to crew on board *Carousel* in the 1964 San Diego to Acapulco Race, which *Carousel* won on corrected time. On board were some top-notch local yachtsmen: Malin Burnham, Bud Caldwell and Jim Reynolds (all of whom would later crew for Conner in the Star class).

Among the lessons Bown imparted to the young sailor was the importance of knowing your boat, preparing it for optimum performance, and selecting a

Courtesy of Dale Frost, Port of San Diego

good helmsman and crew. Conner would learn those lessons well.

The 1960's and '70's also brought fame to another sailor and local boatbuilder Carl Eichenlaub.

Though Eichenlaub had been building boats since 1951 at his yard on Shelter Island, it was not until Lowell North won three Star World Championships and the Gold Medal in the 1968 Olympics on boats built by Eichenlaub, that Eichenlaub gained his reputation as the best Star builder in the world. At one time, Eichenlaub Stars held national titles in five nations simultaneously. During that time, Eichenlaub had also built a series of championship Snipes and Solings. The number of winning boats and the types of boats built become sketchy, as Eichenlaub admits:

"We've kept lousy records, that's one thing I've often kicked myself about. I couldn't tell you how many boats we've built here or for whom we've built them."

As the string of successes in boatbuilding lengthened, so did the list on Eichenlaub's own sailing record. By the 1960's, he had already won the International 14, Sabot and Skimmer Class Championships before going on to win two Lightning National titles and the World Cup, not to mention a host of other top rankings in several other classes.

Eichenlaub was invited by the U.S. Olympic Committee to act as the official shipwright for four Olympic games: 1976 in Munich, 1980 in Moscow (in which the U.S. did not participate), 1984 in Los Angeles and 1988 in Korea. His job involved maintaining the U.S. boats and repairing any damage to them during the games.

In 1972, a 27-year-old man walked into Eichenlaub Marine, inquiring about the cost of building a boat which he had designed. Eichenlaub gave him the estimate, which sent the young designer dejectedly back to

Courtesy of Howard Thomas

This historic shot was taken in 1973 by Dr. Nierenberg, director of Scripps Institution of Oceanography. From left to right are Drake and Lance Thomas, Charles Lindbergh, Captain Howard Thomas and Arthur Godfrey.

This image marks the memorable occasion when Charles Lindbergh returned to San Diego with Arthur Godfrey, for the purpose of furthering an environmental impact study on San Diego Bay. Jets roared in the background as they took off from Lindbergh Field, and for those few moments, the past and present were inextricably linked.

This 1959 photo places Ash Bown on board his 40' Owens Cutter Carousel, which he sailed to many first place finishes. Local sailors remember him as being a "seat of the pants sailor," which might be interpreted as having a mixture of innate sailing ability, common sense and a winning spirit.

Courtesy of San Diego Historical Society, Union Tribune Collection

his drawing board. Without any financial backing to shore him up, the designer thought that if he could scale down the size of the boat, perhaps he could scale down the cost of building it. With a new, smaller design in hand, the young man returned to Eichenlaub for a second estimate. The estimate was still out of reach, so he asked Eichenlaub:

"What's costing so much?" Eichenlaub told him it was the cost of the

Neva Sullaway

doors and drawers, to which the young man answered: "Fine, I'll design a simple boat with no drawers, no doors and no nothing."

That "simple boat," christened *Ganbare*, would become legendary. The young designer, Doug Peterson, would suddenly be launched into the forefront of yacht design. Carl Eichenlaub, as the boat's builder, would be inundated with orders for Peterson designs.

Admittedly, *Ganbare* was not the most finished looking boat. Built in an incredible seven weeks, the wooden-hulled boat was completed just in time for the 1973 One-Ton Nationals sailed in San Diego. No one particularly recognized the 34' *Ganbare* as posing a threat, especially with her paint peeling away as she made her way to the starting line. She was so unconventional looking that neither Dennis Conner nor

Carl Eichenlaub, at the wheel of his 45-footer Cadenza *(sail #47774), continues his racing career on San Diego Bay. Eichenlaub possesses a rare combination of skills: master craftsman, boatbuilder and world class sailor, as well as being an accomplished musician. When he is not racing or helping someone with their own boat project, Eichenlaub will most likely be found in his shed at Eichenlaub Marine, fairing the curves on his newest boat.*

Neva Sullaway

A Winning Boat is Priceless

Lowell North were much interested in racing *Ganbare* – not interested, that is, until *Ganbare* left everyone at the starting gate! At that time, *Ganbare* was up against the latest in Gary Mull and Bruce King designs. Top ranking sailors were also among the fleet, with Ted Hood racing his own design, *Robin*, and Ted Turner on the S&S 38 *Bullet*.

After winning the U.S. One-Ton Championships, *Ganbare* went on to place second in the Worlds, after being penalized for rounding a mark the wrong way. It was an unfortunate error, which the sailors on board (Lowell North, Gary Wiseman, John Driscoll, Ron Holland, Doug Peterson, Scott Kaufman and Bill Green) could have easily kept to themselves, as there was no one near them to witness the event. However, being sailors of integrity, they reported the incident and took the penalty.

Overwhelmed with orders to build Peterson designs, Eichenlaub produced seven One-Tonners, two Quarter-Tonners and a Quarter-Ton plug in just over a year! Peterson's list of winning offshore designs in the latter part of the '70's became too lengthy to tally. On the long list are S.O.R.C and Admiral's Cup wins with several One-Ton and Half-Ton Cups to his credit.

During the 1970's and 1980's, Peterson produced such winning names as *Magic Twanger*, *Louisiana Crude*, *Scarlett O'Hara*, *Lively*, *Pied Piper* (Lowell North), *Stinger* and *High Roler* (Dennis Conner), *Vendetta* and Peterson's own *Flambuoyant*.

Jeffrey Hunter

The 41' aluminum-hulled sloop Flambuoyant *was built by Eichenlaub Marine, and is currently skippered by Doug Peterson.* Flambuoyant *won the San Diego Ocean Racing Fleets 1990 season.*

After twenty years of producing successful designs, it was not surprising that Peterson became involved in the design of the new International America's Cup Class sloop for the Beach Boys syndicate (later absorbed by the America[3] syndicate). Other members of the design team include John Reichel and Jim Pugh.

Quintessence, a Reichel/Pugh 42 owned by Don Hughes of the Santa Barbara Yacht Club, won the overall IOR division of the 1990 Hot Rum series. Quintessence *is also the 1989 winner of the Ahmanson Series (Newport Beach), Long Beach Race Week and Yachting Cup (San Diego).*

Reichel/Pugh designs, which began appearing on the racing circuit in the mid-1980's with Blade Runner, *keep re-appearing in the headlines.* Abracadabra's *recent win in the 1991 50' World Cup Series Championships capped a successful racing season for Reichel/Pugh's first 50' design launched in March 1990.*

Jeffrey Hunter

America's Cup History

1960-1983

Columbia prepared for her next bid for the Cup by training against *Newsboy* in Newport Beach. The team of Gerry Driscoll, Lowell North, Gene Trepte (Chairman of the 1992 America's Cup Defense Committee), Rodney Hughes and Joe Jessop worked through 1965, '66 and '67 readying themselves and the boat for the 1967 Cup Defense trials. After a reorganization, only Joe Jessop, as team manager, ended up joining the new mix of sailors (which included Bill Ficker) on board *Columbia*. Joe Jessop acted as the trial horse skipper that year, pacing *Weatherly* against *Columbia*.

Olin Stephens' new 12-Meter *Intrepid* was preparing for her own defense of the Cup. With a revolutionary design, including a separate rudder, trim tab and most winches below deck, *Intrepid* handily won in 1967. Stephens was always one step ahead of the game.

Driscoll remained undaunted by the disappointments of 1967, and attempted a new campaign with *Intrepid* in 1974. Between 1971 and 1974, Driscoll's boatyard worked persistently on *Intrepid's* design, trying to eliminate every ounce of extra weight while maintaining the boat's integrity. The

Courtesy of San Diego Maritime Museum

The launching of the rebuilt Columbia (1958 America's Cup winner) at Driscoll's Boatyard in San Diego was a portentous moment in San Diego's sailing history. It would bring the first 12-Meter to San Diego waters and local interest in the America's Cup event would heighten considerably. Columbia would also link Gerald Driscoll with the acclaimed designer Olin Stephens.

▼

Two classic yachts met on San Diego waters in 1973. The 1967 America's Cup winner Intrepid came out to greet the 1904 steam yacht Medea upon her arrival in San Diego. In the following year, under the helmsmanship of Gerry Driscoll, Intrepid would live up to her name in the America's Cup trials.

Courtesy of San Diego Maritime Museum

Bob Grieser

Bob Grieser

result of this extreme weight-loss program left *Intrepid* 4,000 lbs. lighter! Though the older, wooden-hulled *Intrepid* would ultimately be defeated by the new aluminum *Courageous* in the trials, *Intrepid* stunned her adversaries with her speed over the course.

Now at an age when most men edge into retirement, Driscoll has undertaken one of the most ambitious projects of his lifetime – the rebuilding of his yard on Shelter Island. When the announcement of the venue for the 1992 America's Cup sent foreign syndicates in search of a land base for their operations, Driscoll's boatyard provided an ideal location. Mutually agreeable plans for a completely new boatyard were drawn up between the Italian syndicate and Driscoll, and, with the final approval of the San Diego Unified Port District, the 50-year-old yard made way for the new.

For the 1977 Cup Races, Lowell North and Malin Burnham teamed up and brought *Enterprise* to the West Coast for training. Their efforts were dashed when *Courageous* was again selected to defend. Gregarious skipper Ted Turner took the helm of *Courageous* and soundly defeated Alan Bond's *Australia* 4-0.

By 1980, the approach to America's Cup racing was facing a new era of challenges. Most notably, Dennis Conner had entered the arena as a skipper. He entered it with the same obsession as a Lipton, with skills surpassing Vanderbilt's and with the absolute dedication of an Olympic sportsman. The San Diego sailor would leave his indelible mark on the history of the America's Cup, changing it forever.

By the 1980's, the Cup's list of foreign challengers was expanding, with Alan Bond driving the Australians into the

Rosenfeld Collection, Mystic Seaport Museum

EASTERLY
SAN DIEGO, CA

Bob Covarrubias

Bob Covarrubias

Bob Covarrubias

After their move west, the Sutphens brought out their own classic yacht from Bar Harbor, Maine. The 38' Easterly is a lobster boat hull beautifully finished as a yacht.

high-tech era, and France and England becoming increasingly competitive. Yet it was Dennis Conner who sailed 44 races in the 1980 trials, tallying 40 wins! In the finals against Bond's *Australia*, Conner would dominate again with a 4-1 score.

The 1980 Cup races demonstrated what an intensive year-round training program can accomplish. Conner trained by matching *Enterprise* against *Freedom* for eighteen solid months of sailing, which were split between summer sailing off Newport, Rhode Island, and winter practice off San Diego.

In 1979, one of Conner's secret training weapons arrived in Newport, Rhode Island, from Larchmont, New York, in the form of a seemingly mild-mannered ex-sailmaker named Jack Sutphen. Sutphen's own career spanned forty years of sailing, in the top echelon of East Coast racing; this included almost every America's Cup since 1958, as either a sailmaker or crew member. Sutphen has sailed on

Sutphen has been classified by Dennis Conner as being one of the best skippers in the world, in terms of straight line sailing. The job of a trial horse skipper is one of being able to get the maximum effort out of his boat on any given course, day after day, with a high degree of consistency.

In 1983, Liberty and Freedom (Conner's 1980 winner) prepared for battle on San Diego waters. San Diegans would become more involved with the America's Cup, as it became a full-time endeavor for local sailors. Many of the crew members would hail from San Diego or eventually transfer from the East Coast to make San Diego their home.

A Winning Boat is Priceless

► *By 1983, Conner had won two Star Worlds (1970 and '77, the latter with the series' only perfect score, 5-0) and a bronze medal in Tempests in the 1976 Olympics. He had skippered three boats to overall victories in the SORC series and Conner was a Congressional Cup winner.*

fourteen 12-Meter yachts over the years, a record unrivaled by his sailing peers. After the 1979 winter training program in San Diego, Sutphen and his wife, Jean, settled in San Diego permanently.

Conner met Sutphen in 1974 on board *Courageous*, and after having recognized the sailor's talent, Conner signed him on as trial horse skipper for the 1980, '83 and '87 America's Cup campaigns; 1992 will again find Sutphen involved in Dennis Conner's bid for a successful defense of the Cup.

Bob Covarrubias

Stanley Rosenfeld, Rosenfeld Collection, Mystice Seaport Museum

 Australia II brought skipper John Bertrand, designer Ben Lexcen and financier Alan Bond into the winners' circle. The battle of boats, skippers and crews had expanded dramatically to include the battle of technologies.

The "Auld Mug" was finally unbolted from the New York Yacht Club's trophy case and sent to Perth, Western Australia, where the 1987 America's Cup was sailed. It was in Perth that the Cup took on a new luster.

▼ *The winged keel, designed by Australian Ben Lexcen, was the focus of controversy throughout the summer of 1983. The boat's performance appeared to give Australia II the edge, while the keel, concealed on land, gave the Australians a decided psychological advantage over the Americans.*

Stanley Rosenfeld captured the winged keel at the moment of its unveiling after the final 1983 match.

Rosenfeld Collection, Mystic Seaport Museum

Shortly after Renegade's *launching in 1978, the young crew of SDYC members, including designer Bruce Nelson and owner Sandy Purdon, headed off on the 1,200-mile San Diego to Manzanillo Race.* Renegade *revelled in the spinnaker runs. Her pronounced overhanging stern transformed increased wetted length into increased speed. Her sixty-foot mast carried more sail area than most boats her size, and gave her a leading edge.*

Chapter Nine

Racing Into the 1990's

1978

◆

When one steps inside the office of Nelson/Marek Yacht Design they get an immediate sense of the intensity of the profession. Their eye is first drawn to the multi-colored computer screen, which displays a yacht-to-be in its most minimalistic form. A computer model, made up of a complex matrix of lines, can be reconstructed by the mere flick of a pen-like "mouse" across the control panel. At a second glance, one is amazed at how small the work space is, considering the volume of designs produced from this office on Shelter Island.

A fully computerized approach has become an essential part of today's yacht design. In light of this approach, it might be interesting to take a small detour, through the side-alleys of history, to the backyard of the San Diego Sports Arena in 1977!

Courtesy of Sandy Purdon

Renegade showed off her beautiful woodwork, which accentuated her well-defined lines as she lay alongside the San Diego Yacht Club's dock. Renegade, whose name defined the people involved in her design and building, was the second Nelson-designed yacht on San Diego Bay.

The area was made up of industrial sites, which attracted carpenters, woodworkers and machinists, looking for a work space at reasonable rates. If one wandered around behind the Sports Arena, along Hancock Street, they were met by a heady whiff of epoxy, and getting close to Geraghty Marine. One look inside the boatbuilder's shed would have been enough; the floor was thick with sawdust and there were piles of lumber strewn everywhere. The long-haired fellow over in the corner holding the plans for the boat under construction seemed totally oblivious of the dust, dirt and general disorder. It didn't matter to him, this was his first commissioned project as a yacht designer...and he was destined to be one of the best.

Bruce Nelson was just out of college, having made his way west. Sandy Purdon, then 35 years old and sporting a moustache and a head of wild curly hair, wanted to have a new boat built which would function not only as a performance racer but also would incorporate comfort for long-distance racing.

By the time the two young men met in San Diego, Nelson, in his early twenties, had only one other boat to his credit. It's an unlikely success story, which began in a pick-up truck in Texas.

While driving back to California after an unsuccessful bid for the 1976 Quarter-Ton World Championships, Nelson bet his sailing buddies that he could design a winning boat, if they would back the building of it. With the aid of a hand-held calculator, Nelson managed to design *Blivit*, the winner of the 1978 Quarter-Ton North Americans.

As bets go, Nelson came to the table with an impressive list of credentials. From an early age, Nelson was greatly influenced by his grandfather, Leroy Grumman, the renowned aircraft designer/builder. Aside from an early start in sailing, which put Nelson on the helm at 10 years of age, Nelson had graduated from the University of Michigan's Naval Architecture school. By the time he was a college graduate, he was already a three-time All-American collegiate sailor. The odds were definitely in Nelson's favor.

The launching of Sandy Purdon's 37-footer *Renegade* set a new course for Nelson. He founded his yacht design company in 1978, and has been holding a steady course since then.

Renegade did go on to many first-place finishes with two successive wins in the San Francisco Perpetual Challenge (1978 and '79). In 1980, *Renegade* became the first foreign yacht to win the Mexican Ocean Racing Circuit. Purdon continued to campaign *Renegade* successfully throughout the 1980's and, like Bruce Nelson, would become an integral part of the successful 1987 America's Cup Challenge. (Purdon was the Executive Director for the Sail America Foundation from 1984-1987.)

Geraghty Marine, as boatbuilders, led the way into the 1980's by constructing an impressive list of high-performance ocean racers.

1980's

◆

Currently on board with Nelson is his partner, Robb Walker, and associates Greg Stewart and Scott Vogel. (Bruce Marek left the design team in 1987.) The future looks particularly exciting for the small company. While being deeply involved in the 1987, 1988 and 1992 America's Cup designs, Nelson/Marek has numerous other projects on the drawing board. They range from 100' performance cruisers to the latest in I.M.S racers, and include the eye-catching 52-foot International Formula-One Class, which is ready to pace the world's top-flight skippers on an international Grand Prix racing circuit. Dennis Conner, Australian Peter Gilmour and German Berend Beilken are among the new class contenders.

By the mid-1980's, Bruce Nelson and his partner Bruce Marek had reason to toast their success. With a margarita in hand, the design team cheered on Nick Frazee's Swiftsure III, which would take its share of the line honors in both Mexico and Transpac races.

Bob Covarrubias

Neva Sullaway

◄ The list of winning designs by Nelson/Marek becomes too lengthy to mention, as hundreds of their boats sail and race worldwide.

San Diego waters found three Nelson/Marek designs all vying for first place in the 1988 Sunkist American Cancer Society Yacht Race: Les Crouch's 69' Maverick (red hull), Mitchell Rouse's 68' Barracuda (to port of Maverick) and George Folgner's Swiftsure III.

► On an average race day on San Diego Bay, a large percentage of the racers are from the Nelson/Marek design table. Carl Eichenlaub's 45' Cadenza is among the leaders in the I.O.R division, along with Bill Bannasch's Eclipse (N/M 43) and the Nelson/Marek 41' Reliance.

Jeffrey Hunter

Jeffrey Hunter

▼ East Coast-based marine photographer Sharon Green followed the action during Audi Yachting Race Week (1990) in Key West, Florida. The Nelson/Marek 46' Collaboration had only been in the water one month before she starting sweeping the I.M.S (International Measurement System) circuit.

▲ Previously owned by Dennis Conner, and named Boat of the Year in 1984, Reliance is currently owned and skippered by Chuck Nichols. The 1985 and 1988 Lipton Cup winner continues her successful career in the I.O.R division, taking home her share of the trophies each year.

Sharon Green

America's Cup History

1984-1988

In retrospect, it seems as if all the necessary forces had been gathering over the years, until the momentum was finally great enough to carry San Diego to the forefront of sailing history. The sailors, the designers, the builders and the entrepreneurs had formed a solid nucleus, and it was only a matter of time before the America's Cup belonged to San Diego.

Bob Covarrubias

◄

Conner's training program for the 1987 America's Cup began as early as 1985, when Liberty and Stars & Stripes '85 match raced on San Diego Bay. Training exercises would eventually move to Hawaiian waters, where the conditions more closely approximated those of Western Australia.

Three versions of *Stars & Stripes* evolved through the design efforts of Britton Chance, David Pedrick and Bruce Nelson, in conjunction with a unique San Diego-based high-technology firm, Science Applications International Corporation (SAIC).

After the Australians defeated the U.S. in 1983, the U.S. Navy became so intrigued by the possible defense and commercial applications of the winged keel that it commissioned SAIC to study the design. The revelations forthcoming from SAIC scientists drew Dennis Conner and Malin Burnham (president of the Sail America Foundation) into the inner circle of America's technologically elite.

Bob Covarrbias

SAIC's chief executive officer, Dr. J. R. Beyster, committed the company's resources as well as providing initial funding in 1984. The job of coordinating the bold new approach, which included East and West Coast research facilities, went to John Marshall. Marshall's qualifications included being a world-class sailor with 12-Meter experience and the ability to speak two languages fluently – sailing and computer.

In the fast-paced 1980's, computers were no longer landlubbers. On-board instrument sailing became the norm. The intuitive questions of how far to sail on a "header" and when to tack were replaced by the digitally recorded information of exactly how many degrees the header had knocked you from your preset course, and how much boat speed you had lost from the prescribed optimum. All the necessary information was displayed in front of you at any given moment.

The largest exponential component for winning was still the man and his machine.

Stanley Rosenfeld,
Rsenfeld Collection,
Mystic Seaport Museum

In the end, *Stars & Stripes* '87 was the result of a mammoth joint effort, in which computer analysis and simulations (such as the Velocity Prediction Program) played a key role. There were thousands of VPP runs (which predicted the optimum sailing angle and speed for any combination of wind speed and heading), hundreds of hours of computer flow code analysis, thirty-three model tests and four full-size boats for trial. American ingenuity was a principal player in the race to recapture the America's Cup.

Dale Frost, Port of San Diego

Conner brought the Cup home via airplane, with the Cup strapped into a first-class seat next to him. The America's Cup sailors arrived to a hero's welcome, as over 60,000 San Diegans turned out to greet them. Both Malin Burnham and Dennis Conner were overwhelmed at the reception; after all, it had been a long haul to the finish line.

As the triumphant skipper, Conner had a long list of people to thank, among them his exemplary crew. On board were Peter Isler (San Diego), Jon Wright, Adam Ostenfeld, James Kavle, Bill Trenkle (San Diego), Jay Brown, Henry Childers, John Barnitt, Scott Vogel (San Diego) and tactician Tom Whidden. To follow was an even longer list of supporters, which was topped by Malin Burnham's Sail America Foundation, and the illustrious trial horse crew, the "Mushrooms," headed by Jack Sutphen.

The era of 12-Meters was coming to an end, faster than anyone could have imagined. Within six months, New Zealand merchant banker Michael Fay came to San Diego and laid a completely new challenge on the table. Within nineteen months, a whole new version of America's Cup racing took place off San Diego's Point Loma. Technology, the men, and their boats hurled everyone into a future that no one seemed quite prepared for.

Bob Covarrubias

The America's Cup event held in 1988 was almost a paper race. Most of the pre-race training took place in the courtroom as this photo by Dale Frost, courtesy of the Port of San Diego, attests. At first, the legitimacy of the challenge was questioned, then the boats, then the races, then the winner...until the Cup itself was carted off to a high security vault in New York.

Bob Grieser

▲
With little time available to design, test and build a monohull with a maximum waterline length of 90', the Americans opted for the fastest hull shape, given the limitation of waterline length. The result of the design team and SAIC's efforts rendered the theoretically fastest hull shape – an ultra-light 60' catamaran. Hard wing and soft wing sails were designed for the catamaran, offering two highly efficient options.

There are very few photos of the event that managed to get both yachts in the same picture – the catamaran was simply too fast.

As in the entire history of the America's Cup, whenever the dust settled after a controversy, a new horizon became visible; it happened in 1871 when the word "match" (as in match race) was disputed, just as it happened in the 1980's. Ultimately, the controversy served to heighten competition, not lessen it. As a result of the battles waged in 1988-89, the 1992 America's Cup offers an exciting new International America's Cup Class monohull sloop (75' LOA), a new race course (which will put the sailors and their boats to the ultimate test), and a broader field of challengers, which includes the world's best sailors.

Dale Frost, Port of San Diego

While Conner signed on such sponsors as Merrill Lynch, Pepsi and Marlboro, Michael Fay captured the limelight when his team sailed New Zealand down the center of the bay during the 1988 Sunkist American Cancer Society Cup Race, scheduled just two weeks before the start of the America's Cup races.

◀

Neva Sullaway

▲
New Zealand dwarfed every boat in the harbor, including Roy Disney's Pyewacket (NM 70). Fay proved himself to be the ultimate showman, while managing to raise an additional $5,000 for the American Cancer Society.

It was hard not to be impressed by the sheer magnitude of the Bruce Farr-designed 132' New Zealand, which carried a crew of thirty-five men. The mast alone stood fifteen stories high and carried one-third of an acre of sail!

Bob Covarrubias

The Cup has stood through a century and a half untarnished, proudly attesting to a sporting tradition, which drove men to achieve more than seemed possible; and so it will again.

Dale Frost, Port of San Diego

Best captioned as "Goodbye America," Michael Fay and his crew prepared for their departure from San Diego waters. On the race course, Dennis Conner and his crew had dispatched the Kiwis in two decisive victories. The paper race, however, was still on. The final court decision was handed down in late April of 1990. The legitimacy of the 1988 races was upheld and the America's Cup was allowed to come home.

The 27th running of the America's Cup spanned the gamut of public emotion. Among seasoned sailors, there was a sense of outrage that two such different boats were expected to sail a fair race. Then there was the majority of spectators in the middle, who were simply befuddled by both apparitions. At the farthest extreme, there was a small minority who tried to maintain their sense of humor about it all.

Bob Covarrubias

1990's

◆

An interesting outcome of the 1988 America's Cup competition was the demonstration of the impressive performance capabilities of the catamaran. Multihulls (including both catamarans and trimarans) have often been overlooked in historical accounts, largely because of the monohull's traditional hold on both the cruiser and racing divisions. However, the concept of a multihulled craft (paddled or sailed) is as old as the concept of outrigger canoes, which have been used for centuries.

Courtesy of Mark Gumprecht

▲

Mark Gumprecht sails his Cross-design Trick *on San Diego Bay.*

San Diego was the home of the internationally respected multihull designer Norman Cross (1915-1990). As a member of the San Diego Yacht Club, Cross often raced his 32' trimaran *Crossfire*, gathering many line honors over the years. Considered the "father of multihulls," the former design engineer for General Dynamics-Convair Division designed and built trimarans in San Diego for thirty-five years. One of the last multihulls to come from Cross's design table is a tribute to his life's work.

Working closely with Cross over a period of four years, marine carpenter and boatbuilder Mark Gumprecht constructed his cold-molded epoxy 41' trimaran hull, adding his own unique rotating mast system, which supports a fully battened main and the headsail. This combination has given his cruiser *Trick* the edge on speed performance.

▼

The trailerable F-27 is fast proving to be a popular boat worldwide!

Paul Kennedy

Belying an old misconception about trimarans with inhabitable interiors, Gumprecht has handcrafted a beautifully customized interior using ash and walnut woods.

A Chula Vista company, Corsair Marine Inc., has attracted the attention of the sailing world by producing the revolutionary F-27 trimaran. With a boat length of 27' overall, the innovative racer/cruiser can be trailered behind a standard car to any favorite sailing location. The trimaran's outboard floats fold up for trailering, decreasing the boat's beam from 19' to 8' 5". The rigging and launching process has been clocked at twenty minutes for one person progressing at a comfortable pace.

The F-27, launched in 1985, was designed by New Zealander Ian Farrier (he is currently San Diego based) and first developed by him in Australia. The craft has since proven its strength and speed against multihulls and monohulls around the world. Among its newsworthy finishes, the F-27 won the 1990 Australian Multihull Offshore Championships, twice finishing ahead of a 60' racing catamaran! Locally, eight of the top twelve places in the multihull division of the Newport-Ensenada Race (1989) were secured by F-27's. The top finishers, led by John Walton on *Corsair* and Dave Hahn on *Super Fox*, corrected out over Dennis Conner.

The F-27 has also successfully completed transatlantic and transpacific crossings, which tested its long range durability. As of January 1991, the thriving young company celebrated the launching of its 200th boat.

I n the world of high performance custom yachts, San Diego's Esprit Racing Yachts/Avion Dynamics Corporation has entered the international arena of advanced composite manufacturing of racing yachts. This highly specialized approach to boat construction, and the manufacturing of composite parts, is a technology being developed by only a handful of yacht builders worldwide.

▼
Esprit Racing Yachts constructed various components for the Stars & Stripes '88 catamaran. On the racing circuit, boats built by Esprit have proven their worth with Taxi Dancer *(Reichel/Pugh 68, pictured),* Sidewinder *(R/P 44) and* Quintessence *(R/P 42) consistently arriving in first place.*

Geri Conser

With an overview of sailing in San Diego, there seems to be an uncommon proportion of resident sailing champions. Whether it is due to the strong and enduring traditon of San Diego's fine yacht clubs, or the testy wind conditions (which make the sport everyman's game), San Diego has become the training ground for the world's best. Whatever the ingredients, San Diego continues that traditon today, with top-ranking sailors from all quarters of the sailing world. Some sailors pursue America's Cup racing – such as Dennis Conner, and former San Diegans Paul Cayard (sailing for the Italian syndicate) and Olympic Gold Medalist Rod Davis (sailing for New Zealand in 1992); others test their skills on home waters or on the ocean racing circuit.

A common denominator among sailors who excel at each level seems to be a strong one-design racing background.

Neva Sullaway

In a class all their own, wavesailors revel in windy spring conditions off North Pacific Beach.

San Diego's Mission Bay was one of the first racing locations for the original Windsurfer One-Design class. The sport has grown dramatically over the years, and encompasses the spectrum of sailing from one-design course racing to breathtaking wavesailing in the surf.

Heading the lengthy list of San Diego sailors who continue their own successful sailing campaigns are Olympic Gold Medalist Robbie Haines (winning the gold in 1984 with Rod Davis and Eddie Trevelyan in Solings), Mark Reynolds, Vince Brun, Hugo Schreiner, J.J. and Peter Isler, Brian Ledbetter and Mike O'Bryan, to name just a few. Such a list, of course, can never be complete. For almost every skipper there is a crew, and for every crew a support team, whether it be family or an America's Cup syndicate.

This pictorial history celebrates the continuing legacy passed from one sailor to another, and from one generation to the next. Just as Clem Stose took Ash Bown on the Honolulu Race in 1926, and Ash Bown took Dennis Conner along on the Acapulco Race in 1964, one can be sure there is a young sailor scuffing his deck shoes along the docks waiting for his turn to set sail.

San Diego was well represented in 1988 by a six-member Olympic sailing team. From left to right are sailors Hugo Schreiner, Brian Ledbetter, Vince Brun, J.J. Isler, Mike O'Bryan and Mark Reynolds.

Three-time Soling World and Star World champion Vince Brun has signed on as crew on board Team Dennis Conner's Stars & Stripes '92.

Bob Covarrubias

Mark Reynolds, 35, has put in his share of hours on the water. Starting in the SDYC Junior Program at age 8, Mark was inspired by some of the sailing greats around him: Ash Bown, Dennis Conner, Malin Burnham and Peter Bennett, and, not least among them, his own father and avid Star sailor Jim Reynolds.

The San Diego Yacht Club lays claim to another accomplished skipper, Jennifer "J.J." Isler. J.J. (from the Fetter family, the current owners of Kettenburg Marine) credits the strong emphasis on racing in the Junior Program for providing her with the early skills which have guided her through a highly competitive sailing career. Instructor Mark Reynolds helped sharpen the racing skills of her sabot class, which included current Finn Champion Brian Ledbetter.

Bob Covarrubias

While J.J. trained for the Olympic Trials (with crew Amy Wardell) in 1987, husband Peter played a key role in the triumphant 1987 (and 1988) America's Cup Challenge, serving as navigator on board Stars & Stripes. Together and apart, J.J. and Peter logged 320 days of sailing throughout 1987!

While at Yale, J.J. was the first female Varsity Team Captain, and in 1985 she was the only female named to the prestigious Collegiate All-American team. J.J. continued her intensive sailing campaign after her college years, winning the 1986 470 European Championships and the IYRU Women's World Championships. J.J. was named Rolex Yachtswoman

Bob Covarrubias

of the Year in 1987, and with her strong female crew, won the Rolex International Keelboat Championships that same year. J.J. is currently training for the 1992 Olympics.

Courtesy of the Fetter family

Mark Reynolds's list of national and international victories, covering twenty-six years of top level competition, is impressive. In the 1980's alone, Reynold's wins included the 1986 Goodwill Games, and the 1987 USYRU Match Racing Championships, followed by a second in the Star Worlds and a Silver Medal in the 1988 Olympics in Pusan, Korea.

While Reynolds fixes his sight on the 1992 Olympics, his Shelter Island sailmaking loft, Sobstad, continues to turn out award-winning sails.

The San Diego Yacht Club, trustee of the America's Cup, carries on a proud sailing tradition.

dewitt '91

Chapter Ten

At the Sound of the Gun!

1990's

◆

he 1990's will provide some thrilling moments in San Diego's sailing history. The spotlight will be the brightest at the start of America's Cup racing.

Bob Grieser

OFFICE OF THE COMMODORE
SAN DIEGO YACHT CLUB

H.P. "SANDY" PURDON
COMMODORE

Organized in 1886, the San Diego Yacht Club has been blessed with over a century of sailing, which has extended from San Diego Bay to numerous ports around the world. Participation in sailing has taken the San Diego Yacht Club from its modest beginnings to a status of grand accomplishments and important responsibilities.

The ocean has an important message. Those of us who crave time on the water know that the ocean will humble even the most skilled and experienced sailor at some point.

The mettle of the sailor is his ability to muster the internal fortitude to come back and successfully overcome a setback. Challenges arise everywhere on the water, and sailors relish those moments of personal victory.

San Diego Yacht Club members have been able to translate the skills of a yachtsman into successful accomplishments both on and off the water. The fiber of San Diego's community leadership is interwoven throughout the Yacht Club's history. We like to think the sport of sailing builds into the character of man the attention to detail and humility of purpose, which are necessary ingredients for leadership.

Only with an overview of our impressive sailing past can we look to the future with great hope and inspiration.

Keep the steady strain,

H.P. "Sandy" Purdon
Commodore

Bob Covarrubias

The America's Cup is an apt symbol for the vibrant, growing city of San Diego. A feeling of excitement emanates along the waterfront, as the city prepares for the start of the twenty-eighth running of the America's Cup races.

One photo, snapped at 1/125th of a second, can record an enormous amount of history. When Malin Burnham and Joe Jessop stopped to chat at the San Diego Yacht Club, photographer Stephen Simpson saved the moment for posterity. Both men are respected community leaders, past Commodores of the SDYC, Star Champions and America's Cup trial skippers.

Against the background of a strong maritime past, San Diego photographers capture those images which illuminate the "Harbor of the Sun." The past and present meld under varying shades of color, projecting a new and undiscovered visage at each glance.

The sails atop the San Diego Convention Center celebrate a nautical heritage with a vantage towards the future.

Stephen Simpson

As dusk settles over the Sagres (a visiting Portuguese sailing ship) faint memories recall those early sailing ships, which breathed the very life into the struggling New Town.

Dale Frost, Port of San Diego

At the Sound of the Gun!

Dale Frost, Port of San Diego

Stephen Simpson

▲

An interesting photographic composition finds a naval ship passing by the impressive bowsprit of the Star of India, a reminder that San Diego is one of the largest naval seaports in the world today.

▲

The movement of ships in and out of the harbor provide spectacular moments.

Stephen Simpson

➤

San Diego is still an active fishing port for both recreational and commerical fishing.

Dale Frost, Port of San Diego

▲

Alonzo Horton might have trouble recognizing the plot of land he deeded to the city of San Diego in 1895. The development of Horton Plaza by Ernest W. Hahn, Inc. (opened in 1985) has proven to be an unprecedented success. The Plaza attracts about 14 million visitors annually – more than any Southern California amusement park!

At the Sound of the Gun!

Of the events that take place around the bay, the arrival of historic sailing ships, such as the Golden Hinde, are momentous occasions.

Sir Francis Drake, British admiral and privateer remembered for his circumnavigation from 1577 to 1580 (the first Englishman to do so), enjoys an occasional voyage to San Diego waters!

Dale Frost, Port of San Diego

San Diego is host to a variety of sailing events, some of which include raising money for such organizations as the American Cancer Society and the Trauma Research & Education Foundation (TREF).

Stephen Simpson

Dale Frost, Port of San Diego

The Race For Life originated in 1987, when Dr. Richard Virgilio on Bravo (46' Kelly/Peterson design) and 1991 Commodore of the San Diego Yacht Club, Sandy Purdon, on Spirit (also a K/P 46), raced single-handed from San Diego to Hawaii in an effort to raise money for TREF. Both sailors were winners in the Race For Life, which raised over $300,000 for the Foundation.

Bob Covarrubias

Dale Frost

Other glimpses around the bay bring to mind the lazy days of summer: the Wednesday night beer can races, early evening breezes and a gentle coast out to the Coronado Islands.

On many weekends, a common sight on the bay is the San Diego Yacht Club's race committee boat, George Kettenburg Jr. Designed by Arthur DeFever, the prominent local designer of luxury motor yachts and fishing vessels, the committee boat also recalls another well-respected yacht designer/builder, George Kettenburg Jr.

The San Diego Yacht Club race committee alone oversees more than 100 official race days a year. The extraordinary skill and dedication of the race committee are essential components in top-level yacht racing.

Eight area yacht clubs provide year-round racing schedules: the San Diego Yacht Club, Southwestern Yacht Club, Silvergate Yacht Club, Kona Kai International Yacht Club, Chula Vista Yacht Club, Coronado Yacht Club, Coronado Cays Yacht Club and Mission Bay Yacht Club.

Neva Sullaway

Dennis Conner, winner of three America's Cup campaigns, finds a few rare moments of relaxation while sailing his Formula 40 catamaran on San Diego Bay. At the age of 49, Conner has already secured his reputation as one of the world's best sailors. The qualities that have marked Conner's successful career are his energy, drive, enthusiasm, dedication, preparation, organization and attention to detail.

Neva Sullaway

Whether harbor-based or ocean racing, San Diego women play an active role in sailing, either as crew or skippers. Tracy Wolf, on board Matt Richter's Impatient, prepares for the start of the 1990 Hot Rum Race.

San Diego has more than its share of female sailing talent. In the forefront are such sailors as Olympic campaigner J.J. Isler, Olympic medalist Annie Nelson, I.O.R. skipper Jean Eichenlaub and 1987 America's Cup trials navigator Dory Vogel (the only woman ever to race on a 12- Meter in an America's Cup trials).

At the Sound of the Gun!

Jeffrey Hunter

Of the ocean races on the Southern California circuit, the Newport-Ensenada and San Diego-Ensenada races bring to the starting line over 450 and 100 racing yachts respectively. The Transpac, San Diego-Manzanillo and Newport-Cabo San Lucas provide longer-distance challenges.

A popular event on the sailing calendar is the annual BMW race. It offers tough competition, attractive awards for the winners and a great party afterwards.

Neva Sullaway

The action is intense but it's not for everyone.

Bob Grieser

Neva Sullaway

Of the fleets that race on the bay, the Etchells provide some of the toughest competition around. Fleet races attract such sailors as Dennis Conner, Bruce Nelson (1990 fleet champion) and Larry Klein (1989 Rolex Yachtsman of the Year and E-22 World Champion).

Neva Sullaway

Photographer Bob Covarrubias went to great heights to achieve a spectacular vantage from above the yards, while crew members on board the Californian secured the topsail. Sail training on board the Californian is one way for young people and adults to share in a unique maritime environment. As an example, the Californian Cadet Program offers students a chance to study earth science, environmental awareness, California history and applied sciences, all interwoven with learning the skills of sailing on board a tall ship.

Bob Grieser

Bob Grieser

Junior sailing programs are an effective way to acquaint young people with the art of sailing. Sailing encompasses much more than simply learning how to move a craft through the water. Young people can gain tremendously from the lessons of the sea in terms of learning self-reliance, concentration, commitment, self-discipline and decision-making skills, while developing agility and confidence in boat-handling. Sailing also offers a great deal of basic fun.

One of the newest classes to make a splash locally are the Lehman 12's. Raced with two people on board, the 12-footer welcomes the sailor back from the high-tech complexities of big boat racing. Perfect for close-quarter maneuvering, the burgeoning class has lured some familiar racing names: Malin Burnham (sail #324), John Burnham, Mark Reynolds, the Driscolls, Sandy Purdon and Dennis Conner.

Dale Frost

Some children become initiated early, like eighteen-month-old Brett Korporaal, son of Keith and Vikki Korporaal (owners of the classic yacht Orion).

Exactly what the America's Cup might mean to different individuals, and to the city of San Diego, was posed to some young students from San Diego's Gompers Secondary School. The school was the recipient of the 1990 California Distinquished School Award. The America's Cup Organizing Committee selected Gompers as the first school to host the Cup and participate in an essay contest.

The following are a few excerpts from some of the winning essays, entitled "What The Cup Means To Me."

Jesse Wesley - 11th Grade:

*"The America's Cup is not only significant to San Diego;
it also has its significance as a treasure to the entire nation.
Ever since 1851, American designs, technology, and sailing skills
have contributed to the astonishing success of the Americans
during each of the races. To the United States of America, the
America's Cup symbolizes a continuous tradition of excellence,
pride and friendly competition."*

Deborah Le - 7th Grade:

*"It just fills my heart with joy just looking at the Cup. This is just
the happiest day of my life....Everybody worked together and gave
their best. It's the spirit of working together and pulling
together that will make this world a better place."*

David Harrison - 9th Grade

*"The America's Cup means a lot to me personally too. I think the
races offer a positive outlet for people who like to compete. I'd much
rather worry about the cut of the Russians' sail than the shape of
their guided missiles. I am inspired by the way Dennis Conner and
the other America's Cup skippers give their all to win. I attach
symbolic significance to their efforts to strive to be the best. The
America's Cup is a symbol. It keeps the congenial competitive spirit
alive in all of us. It helps to encourage striving for progress."*

At the Sound of the Gun!

"Working together" will certainly be the motto of the 1992 America's Cup races. The city of San Diego, Port of San Diego and the America's Cup Organizing Committee will work together to help make San Diego the premier site for the Cup races with all their auxiliary events.

Skippers will work together with their crews and support teams to prepare themselves for months of racing. As never before in the history of the Cup, the American Defenders will work together in a cooperative design effort called PACT (Partnership for America's Cup Technology). Spearheaded by SAIC, the same high-tech firm which contributed to the winning efforts in 1987 and 1988, PACT has become the fulcrum around which the American syndicates have pooled their research and design technology.

John Marshall, general manager of PACT and director of the Cup-winning Stars & Stripes design teams in 1987 and 1988, stated the challenge most succinctly:

"The bottom line is that ultimately, with a tough new class, somebody's going to come up with a better mousetrap, and it better be us."

Stephen Simpson

In its most simplistic form, yacht racing might be considered the ultimate chess match, whereby each calculated move advances the player over a course. Throughout each level of advancement there is a complex series of choices, the sum total of which will declare the player either a winner or a loser. Among the elements that make sailboat racing a more elusive game are the uncontrollable forces it involves – the wind and the sea. Sailors approach sailing with a sense of awe, while harboring that irrepressible desire to match themselves against nature, as well as other opponents.

The "buttonhook" turn at the bottom
leg of the new 22.6 nautical mile
America's Cup race course was to the
1991 World Cup contenders as Cape
Horn is to long distance sailors. The
tight 180° turn was wrought with
potential disaster as the wily 75' IACC
yachts, with their sixteen man crew,
converged at the mark.

Chapter Eleven

Rounding Buttonhook

1991

◆

America's Cup fever swept through San Diego one year earlier than expected. The 1991 International America's Cup Class (IACC) World Championships provided a glimpse of the 1992 sailing spectacular.

From clandestine late night arrivals of the new IACC yachts, to the capricious wind and wave conditions off of San Diego's Point Loma headland, the 1991 World Championships provided a collage of color, action and drama – and a completely new chapter in the history of sailing. An innovative class of ultra-high technology racing yachts, a challenging 8-lap zig-zag race course with hairpin turns, demanding the highest level of sailing skills from both skipper and crew – at the highest price – have changed the course of sailing history.

As a preview of the events surrounding the 1992 America's Cup, the 1991 IACC World Championships brought the first wave of excitement as New Zealand, Italy, Japan, Spain, France and the US set up their base camps for the coming year of Cup racing. A flurry of activity was noticeable all along the waterfront as boatyards were levelled and reconstructed to accommodate the sail lofts, boat cradles, large cranes and operations offices, which were required for more than a year of residence for those countries hoping to unseat the most prized trophy in sailing. At least four more countries are expected to arrive in 1991, posing a formidable threat to America's efforts to retain the Cup.

The America's Cup Organizing Committee, working closely with the San Diego Unified Port District and the city of San Diego, hosted the 1991 World Championships as a dress-rehearsal for 1992. With the opening of the Media Center and Regatta Headquarters at the Convention Center, the America's Cup International Village at the Embarcadero Marina Park North and the America's Cup Museum at the B Street Pier, the round of cultural festivities, educational exhibitions and championship racing brought the spectators out in full force.

Neva Sullaway

▲

The America's Cup Village fielded a consortium of attractions, including a rotunda of historical exhibitions below a multi-colored sail display, an international food court and beer gardens, a large center stage for ongoing entertainment and a Diamondvision TV on a floating barge for viewing the races live.

▼

When the World Championships crossed paths with the all-day Cinco de Mayo celebrations at the Village, sailors and non-sailors packed the arena to enjoy the best of all worlds – music, sailing and sun.

Neva Sullaway

Dale Frost, Port of San Diego

America's Cup team representatives were asked to pose for a "Media Moment," before heading out to the waters off Point Loma for their first taste of world class competition in the newly-designed IACC yachts. From left to right stand: Chris Dixon (Nippon Sailing Team); Buddy Melges, Bill Koch and Gary Jobson (America³); Rod Davis and David Barnes (New Zealand); Paul Cayard (Il Moro di Venezia); Pedro Campos (Spain '92 Quinto Centenario); Marc Pajot (Ville de Paris); John Kolius (Il Moro di Venezia) and John Bertrand (Stars & Stripes).

France

The world's largest cargo plane (the Russian AN-124) arrived in mid-April with the French yacht Ville de Paris on board. Experienced America's Cup skipper, Marc Pajot, lays claim to having won the very first formal race (in the Pre-Worlds Regatta) in the new IACC boats. Impressively, Ville de Paris had only been sailed five times prior to the Pre-Worlds Regatta.

Jeffrey Hunter

Jeffrey Hunter

Dale Frost, Port of San Diego

Jeffrey Hunter

Spain

Spain '92 Quinto Centenario *celebrates Spain's 500th Anniversary of Columbus's discovery of America, and Spain's first entrance in an America's Cup campaign. The skipper of Spain '92, Pedro Campos was greatly encouraged with the team's performance during the World Championships:*

"We have proven we can keep up with the world's top sailors... We're definitely serious about the America's Cup."

U.S.A.

The well-heeled industrialist and president of America³ Foundation, Bill Koch entered the race for the America's Cup with a wealth of select sailing talent and technology, comprising his Defense campaign. Koch exposed the consternation surrounding the new class: "...they [the IACC boats] are a dream for designers and boatbuilders and a nightmare for owners and crews. They cost a fortune to build and they break."

Jeffrey Hunter

Jeffrey Hunter

Dennis Conner, winning America's Cup helmsman in 1980, 1987 and 1988, "came back" with his own carefully culled crew, a growing list of sponsors and a streamlined, midnight-blue hull. After qualifying for the semi-finals with Italy and New Zealand, Conner announced: "I'm not going in the semis...I've accomplished my goals out of this regatta, which were to learn as much as I could about the other guys and let them know as little about our boat as possible."

Neva Sullaway

Japan

Jeffrey Hunter

Though the history of the America's Cup is littered with broken masts, it did not soften the blow when Nippon's 110' carbon-fiber mast exploded into a half-million dollars worth of fragments. The heart-stopping moment intensified concerns over the fragility of the new IACC boats, which are 30% lighter while carrying 40% more sail area than the 12-Meters used in previous Cup racing.

The world's top-ranked match racer and 1987 America's Cup helmsman, New Zealander Chris Dixon, shaped an impressive team for Japan's first campaign for the Cup.

Having suffered the most setbacks in terms of breakages, Dixon was undaunted by the mishaps: "They're [the IACC boats] a challenge to the world's top sailors. They really do require the best of design, construction and sailing team. I really feel they're a fantastic boat to sail and exactly what the America's Cup is all about."

Dale Frost, Port of San Diego

New Zealand

The New Zealand team, headed by the multi-talented "Will Vary," is very clear about their objective – to take home the Cup. Seasoned skipper David Barnes (1988 America's Cup Challenger), Rod Davis (former Coronado resident and Olympic Gold medalist) and Russell Coutts (in the top-four of world match-racers) exchanged time at the helm during the World Championships, finishing second behind ITA-15 in the finals.

Italy

Italian industrialist Raul Gardini heads the Il Moro di Venezia sailing team. With his two boats (ITA-1 and ITA-15) dominating the 1991 IACC World Championships, Mr. Gardini considered the initial victory an important success for his company, Montedison, one of the major chemical companies in the world and the primary sponsor for the syndicate.

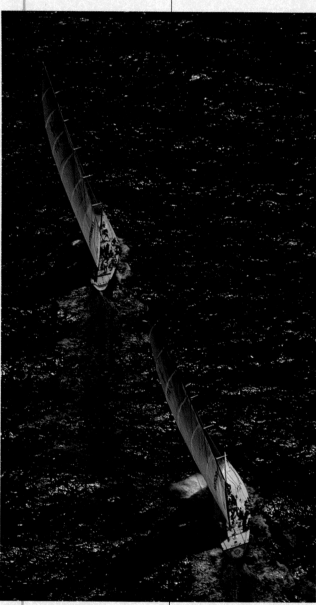

Neva Sullaway

Neva Sullaway

Neva Sullaway

From start to finish, Paul Cayard's ITA-15 was a force to be reckoned with. The Il Moro team had several advantages; among them was time on the water, seemingly unlimited resources and Cayard's skill as a helmsman. Cayard's credentials are lengthy and include being a Star World Champion (1988), Maxi and One-Ton World Champion as well as racing in two previous America's Cup campaigns (1983 Defender and 1987 USA).

Italy-15 *led New Zealand while*
rounding the buttonhook turn.

SAIC: A Profile in High Technology

For more than two decades, employee-owned Science Applications International Corporation (SAIC) has applied its R&D and computer systems expertise to solve complex technical problems for government and commercial clients. Founded by a small group of research scientists in 1969, SAIC has grown into a diversified, high technology company with over 12,000 employees worldwide and annual revenues exceeding $1 billion. SAIC's diverse business base encompasses some 3,000 projects in the areas of national security, energy, environment, health and high technology products.

One example of how SAIC applies the latest technology to tackle complex problems is our America's Cup effort. After the U.S. lost the Cup in 1983, at the request of the Office of Naval Research, SAIC used sophisticated computer programs to show how the winged keel made Australia II faster than Liberty. It became apparent that the America's Cup was no longer only a yacht race, but a technological race as well.

After years of developing state-of-the-art hydrodynamic computer programs for military and commercial vessels, SAIC turned its expertise to 12-Meter yacht design. SAIC scientists developed hydrodynamic codes, which can determine the impact of even a slight design change. In addition, SAIC developed a specialized Velocity Prediction Program (VPP) for 12-Meter design, which allowed designers to predict what each design change meant to overall performance. A race model program we developed enabled scientists to simulate races between two competing boats, under any selected wind, wave and weather conditions. With the help of these technological developments, Stars & Stripes was able to recapture the America's Cup in 1987, and defend it successfully in 1988.

In January of 1990, SAIC organized a high-level research program called the Partnership for America's Cup Technology (PACT) to assist American syndicates who are vying for the Cup in 1992. PACT researchers, including representatives of U.S. technology giants IBM and Boeing, develop new VPPs that predict the speed of candidate designs for America's Cup yachts and perform fluid dynamics calculations that help designers evaluate specific design characteristics. The computer programs used in these calculations are validated and improved through scale model tank testing. PACT makes efficient use of funds by sharing these computer tools with all U.S. syndicates, enabling them to evaluate designs, while building fewer expensive full-scale experimental boats.

SAIC prides itself in applying advanced technology to solve complex problems.

CHCS. Our Composite Health Care System automates and integrates all functions of hospital operations. SAIC is installing CHCS in 750 military medical facilities worldwide.

Spectacular water views abound from every vantage point of the Sheratons on Harbor Island.

The hotels are proud to be an Official Host of the 1992 America's Cup.

OFFICIAL HOST

AMERICA'S CUP '92
SAN DIEGO

ITT Sheraton
HARBOR ISLAND
SAN DIEGO

1380 HARBOR ISLAND DRIVE, SAN DIEGO, CA 92101
PHONE: (619) 291-2900 FAX: (619) 295-5297

Guests of the Sheratons on Harbor Island are dazzled by the striking panoramic views of both the downtown skyline and one of the most beautiful harbors in the world.

Situated on idyllic San Diego Bay, this 1,050 room hotel/resort complex takes full advantage of its unique waterfront setting by offering private sailing charters and whale-watching excursions right from the Sheraton Harbor Island dock.

Two minutes from San Diego International Airport and ten minutes from the city's most famous attractions, the Sheratons on Harbor Island offer an unsurpassed blend of location, service and facilities for vacationers and business travellers alike.

DICK STRATTON:

"A LOCAL CHAMPION"

East Championship in Snipes. After a stint as the National Sailboat Manager for Chrysler Corporation, with offices in Detroit and Dallas, he moved to San Diego in 1971.

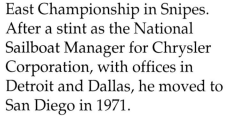

STAR EYED STELLA

There are many levels of competitive sailors in San Diego: America's Cup Champions, World Champions, Olympic Champions, Rock Stars, and "then the rest of us little pebbles," as Dick Stratton states. If it's an Annual Sailing Event in San Diego, Dick Stratton has won it. Dick is a member of Southwestern Yacht Club and has been an active member of the PHRF Fleet for over a decade, as Skipper of *Star Eyed Stella*, *Apollo V*, *Flashdance*, *Lady Godiva*, *The Antares*, and now the only Maxi-Boat berthed in San Diego, *Lady Godiva II* (formerly *Sovereign*).

His many wins include: the New Years Day Race, Charity Bay Race, Valentine's Day Race, Father's Day Race, Fiore Series, Cabrillo Series, SCYA Midwinters, San Diego Yachting Cup, Frazee Series, Marina del Rey/San Diego, Newport/Ensenada, Waterman Series, Arden Series, Hot Rum Series, and the Area G Championship.

Dick also won the San Diego PHRF High Point Championship in 1982, 1983, 1984, and 1985. He won the overall Southern California PHRF Championship in 1983, after finishing third in 1982. His Peterson 25 *Star Eyed Stella* was named *Boat of the Year – 1983* by Southwestern Yacht Club.

Dick started his life of competitive sailing over 35 years ago, sailing Lightnings at the Branford Yacht Club in Connecticut. He competed for Providence College in Ravens, prior to winning the Military All Far

LADY GODIVA

"I am getting a little older and just competed in my third Lipton Cup, so it is time to move on and let the young pebbles take over," says Dick. "I did Carr Cup last year" he continues, "and being Skipper of Victor Fargo's Maxi Lady Godiva II is all the heaven I need."

The Alvarado Hospital Medical Center Campus

Advanced in Care
Advanced in Technology

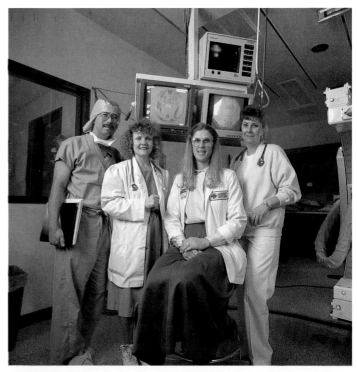

Alvarado Hospital has emerged as a leader in the diagnosis and treatment of cardiovascular disease. More than 400 delicate open-heart surgeries are performed each year. A highly skilled surgical and intensive care nursing team combines "high tech" knowledge with a caring "high touch" approach to cardiac patient care.

Alvarado Hospital's heart catheterization laboratories provide a "high technology" work place for physician specialists and technologists. Diagnostic catheterizations performed here help pinpoint the location of vessel blockages so that the appropriate therapy can begin. In some cases therapeutic procedures using inflatable "balloons" and state-of-the-art lasers help clear arteries without bypass surgery.

Alvarado Hospital Medical Center is one of the largest medical complexes in the San Diego area. Alvarado Hospital is at the hub of this 50-acre site, located between College Avenue and 70th Street near San Diego State University. With 600 physicians on our admitting staff and nearly 1000 supporting employees, the acute care hospital offers general medical and surgical programs, as well as specialized services in cardiac care, orthopedics, women's medicine, oncology and neurosurgery. Complete outpatient services, an up-to-date diagnostic radiology center and emergency department round out our patient care programs.

Arrayed to the east and west of the central hospital are 10 medical buildings. These house the San Diego Sports Medicine Center, Alvarado Convalescent Hospital, Alvarado Parkway Institute's Child and Adolescent Center, San Diego Rehabilitation Institute, and offices for nearly 150 physicians. ■

San Diego Rehabilitation Institute (SDRI)

A free-standing hospital, SDRI is the newest facility on the Alvarado campus. SDRI is committed to one objective: providing the best care and support to patients who face the challenge of physical rehabilitation. SDRI's team of rehabilitation professionals work together using the latest therapeutic techniques to assist each patient in reaching his or her highest potential.

Specialized programs and services include: Brain Injury, Spinal Cord Injury, Stroke, Orthopedics, Pulmonary, Cardiac, Industrial Rehabilitation, Outpatient, Day Treatment and Case Management. ■

Alvarado Parkway Institute's Child and Adolescent Center

The medical campus is also home to Alvarado Parkway Institute's Child and Adolescent Center. This forty-bed facility provides inpatient care for children with emotional and behavioral problems. Alvarado Parkway Institute also manages a separate hospital for adult patients just blocks from the Alvarado campus.

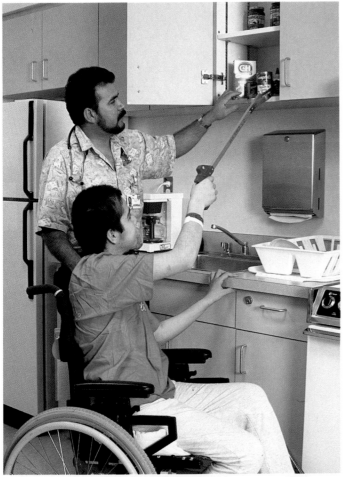

*(Left)
SDRI is focused on providing each patient with the very best care and support as they face the challenge of rehabilitation.*

SDRI has the only transitional living unit in San Diego.

Alvarado Parkway Institute's Child and Adolescent Center offers a safe and supportive home-like setting for inpatient mental health treatment.

As the 21st Century approaches, the Alvarado Hospital Medical Center Campus is well-prepared to meet the total health care needs of its community – through technology, teamwork, dedication and commitment.

*(Right)
SDRI's nurses are always ready to lend a helping hand.*

ALVARADO HOSPITAL MEDICAL CENTER
A National Medical Enterprises Health Care Facility

San Diego Rehabilitation Institute
Focused on the Challenge

API ALVARADO PARKWAY INSTITUTE
CHILD & ADOLESCENT CENTER

Special Acknowledgement to Contributing Photographers

HEATHER HANLEY

STANLEY ROSENFELD:

Renowned maritime photographer Stanley Rosenfeld inherited his great passion for yachting from his father, Morris Rosenfeld (1885-1968). For a century, father and son have been America's premier photographers of steam, power and sailing yachts. The Rosenfeld Collection is housed at the Mystic Seaport Museum, Mystic, Connecticut, and features yacht portraits, harbor scenes and the most complete record of speedboat and sailing races available, including every America's Cup contest since the 1880's.

CHRIS FROST

BOB COVARRUBIAS:

Bob Covarrubias has been a professional photographer specializing in boat portraits (including onboard action, people and yacht racing) for fifteen years. Born and raised in San Diego, Bob has extensively photographed a wide variety of nautical subjects in Southern California. Photographs by Covarrubias have appeared in many national publications and photographic exhibitions.

DENNIS CONNER

DALE FROST:

Dale Frost has been a photographer for the San Diego Unified Port District for more than a decade, chronicling all the maritime activities of the busy Port of San Diego. Dale and her husband, Christopher Frost (owner of Downwind Marine) often enjoy sailing the Frost family's classic yawl *Pacifica*.

STEPHEN SIMPSON:

Stephen Simpson, of Stephen Simpson, Inc., is a twenty-year resident of San Diego and a successful corporate/commercial photographer. Steve works in all formats and his photos reflect a distinctive Simpson trademark of rich color work. Simpson's collection is always expanding as he travels both nationally and internationally to capture images of either personal or commercial value.

BOB GRIESER:

Bob Grieser, born in Washington D.C., is now Chief Photographer for the Los Angeles Times San Diego Edition. Prior to moving west, Bob had spent much time on the Chesapeake Bay sailing and documenting both working and leisure boat activities. Grieser has been a member of the White House News Photographers Association and the National Press Photographers Association. Grieser's work has garnered numerous awards and has been widely published in books and magazines.

CAROLYN KRANTZ-HIRSCHFELD

JEFFREY HUNTER:

Jeffrey Hunter recently returned to San Diego after many years of worldwide travel. His special interest in "photographic adventures" has led him across the continental U.S. as well as many exotic locations, including the Caribbean, Iceland, India, Russia and Hawaii. Hunter's photos have been exhibited across the country and appear regularly in national photographic publications.

Thanks also to contributors:

Sharon Green • Geri Conser • Paul Kennedy

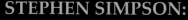

JIM DEWITT
MARINE ARTIST

1232 BRICKYARD COVE ROAD • POINT RICHMOND • CALIFORNIA 94801 • (415) 235-0912

Mercy Healthcare San Diego
Meeting your Healthcare needs.

In 1990, Mercy Hospital celebrated its Centennial anniversary – 100 years of caring for the San Diego community. Today, Mercy Healthcare San Diego continues that tradition of quality care in nearly every medical specialty, from advanced laser surgery to specialized treatment in the home setting. Mercy Hospital also maintains its role as a nationally-recognized teaching facility and an integral part of San Diego County's Trauma System.

CARDIOVASCULAR SERVICES

In 1990, the Mercy Heart Institute added new equipment to aid in the treatment of cardiac disease, including a cardiac mapping computer and devices for precise viewing of the heart and surrounding

Mercy Hospital and Medical Center, founded in 1890, combines state-of-the-art medical treatments with compassionate care.

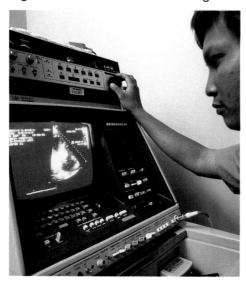

structures in Mercy's three Cardiac Catheterization Laboratories.

Expanding Mercy's comprehensive range of cardiovascular care, a new multidisciplinary Vascular Center opened in September, 1990. A team of physicians skilled in cardiology, radiology and vascular surgery offers expert diagnosis and

Cardiology Technologist Jimmy Phan studies blood flow direction and velocity, using Doppler echocardiography.

prompt referrals for patients with circulatory problems and other vascular disorders.

THE MERCY ORTHOPAEDIC INSTITUTE

Mercy Hospital continues to be the most highly utilized medical center for orthopaedic procedures in San Diego County. The number of back procedures performed at Mercy tripled over the past year,

Wearing special surgical masks, Mercy orthopaedic surgeons perform a total hip replacement procedure in a Laminar Airflow operating room.

and there was also a significant increase in the number of total joint replacements performed at the Hospital. Classes for pre-operative counseling and support of total hip and total knee replacement patients are now held regularly.

Orthopaedic patients also benefit from a computer-assisted design and manufacture system, offering custom-tailored prosthetic devices for total hip implants and amputees.

THE MERCY CANCER CENTER

The Mercy Cancer Center, accredited by the American College of Surgeons, emphasizes patient comfort and convenience through such services as a "satellite" pharmacy located on the Oncology Unit and a comfortable outpatient chemotherapy area. As part of its ongoing patient education efforts, a new Breast Surgery Recovery Program now provides education and referral for women who have had breast surgery.

Ongoing support groups, including the popular "I Can Cope" series and psychological counseling offered through Mercy Behavioral Health, provide education and emotional support to oncology patients and their families.

PULMONARY SERVICES

Plans to expand Mercy's commitment to excellence in pulmonary and critical care medicine will culminate this year in the creation of a Mercy Sleep Disorders Center (for the diagnosis and treatment of sleep disorders) and a Wound Care Outpatient Center (utilizing human growth factors to promote healing in long-term wounds), the only such facility of its kind in San Diego.

THE MERCY NEUROLOGICAL INSTITUTE

Mercy's eight-bed Neurological Intensive Care Unit, created for the skilled medical and nursing supervision of patients recovering from severe neurologic injury or disease, remains the largest unit of its kind in San Diego. The nursing staff's efforts are complemented by state-of-the-art neurologic monitoring

In Mercy's Neurodiagnostics Department an EEG Technician records a patient's brain waves in response to the flashing light. This test helps determine the presence of brain seizure activity.

equipment. Advances in radiologic imaging (such as Magnetic Resonance Imaging and Single Emission Computerized Tomography) offer unprecedented views of the human brain and nervous system. This greatly assists the efforts of Mercy neurologists and neurosurgeons in the diagnosis and treatment of such disorders as strokes, aneurysms, brain tumors and head trauma.

MAGNETIC RESONANCE IMAGING

Magnetic Resonance Imaging (MRI), a valuable diagnostic tool which employs no harmful radiation, continues to expand in use and types of applications. In the Mercy Magnetic Imaging Center, approximately 30 scans (of the brain, knee, limbs, etc.) are performed daily; more than 25,000 MRI studies have been completed since the Center's opening in 1988.

MERCY HOME CARE SERVICES

Mercy Home Care Services offers four major services for patients in the home setting: Home Infusion Therapy (intravenous treatment for antibiotics, chemotherapy and pain management); Medical Equipment (from wheelchairs to walking aids and home oxygen therapy); Certified Nursing (including skilled nursing and social work visits); and Private Duty Nursing (hourly or around-the-clock nursing care).

Also offered is a Pulmonary Specialty program, providing care for patients being treated for obstructive pulmonary or heart disease or asthma, in the home setting. In the HIV Disease Program, specially trained nurses offer comprehensive care for patients with HIV disease. In 1990, Mercy Home Care Services recorded a 40% growth in patient visits over the previous year. ■

A Mercy Home Care nurse provides skilled and compassionate care at her patient's home.

"Race For Life"

Everyday in San Diego dozens of "races for life" involving victims of trauma injuries take place. In 1987 Dr. Richard Virgilio and H.P. "Sandy" Purdon conceived of a **"Race For Life"** to increase awareness of trauma and to benefit the Trauma Research and Education Foundation (TREF). The two yachtsmen challenged each other to a single-handed 2,300 mile race from San Diego across the Pacific to Honolulu, Hawaii. Virgilio, Director of Trauma at Mercy Hospital, began sailing in 1974 with his wife and five children.

Purdon, a former executive director of the Sail America Foundation, began sailing on the east coast when he was nine years old. Both yachtsmen had extensive racing and cruising experience in the waters off California and Mexico and had sailed Transpac before, but never solo. Aboard identical Kelly/Peterson 46's, they faced a variety of physical and mental challenges, and weather and sea conditions in their race, not for the prestige and glory of a particular trophy, but to help save lives. After 16 challenging and often lonely days at sea, Virgilio was the first sailor to finish the race, but the real winners in the **"Race For Life"** were potential trauma victims in San Diego.

In 1988, in an effort to continue to bring the issue of trauma to the public eye, 26 boats, including Dennis Conner and the 1988 America's Cup Catamaran *Stars and Stripes*, joined a **"Race For Life"** around San Diego bay. With proclamations from both the City and County and a spinnaker flying finish creating a colorful scene on the bay, the race attracted much attention and helped raise funds for much needed public education programs on trauma prevention.

In 1989 the **"Race For Life"** broadened to become a bi-annual doublehanded race to Honolulu. Co-hosted as the first regatta was, by the San Diego and Hawaii Yacht Clubs and sponsored by the Hilton Hawaiian Village, the doublehanded Transpac attracted sailors from all

over California. Sailing a Hobie 33, the youngest team, 22-year-old Eric Bohman and 19-year-old Kevin Miller, reached Hawaii after 13 days, two days ahead of their closest competitor.

In July 1991 20 yachts from California, Arizona, Washington and Hawaii will compete in the **"Race For Life"**.

From the initial solo challenge of Purdon and Virgilio to the established doublehanded bi-annual Transpac, the **"Race For Life"** has continued to grow, enjoying the support of the San Diego sailing, medical, and business communities. The generosity and donations of time and resources by the sailors and supporters of the **"Race For Life"** enable TREF to continue it's public and professional education and awareness programs with the goal of preventing trauma deaths in San Diego. ∎

TRAUMA

It's Preventable.

San Diego's Trauma System spans the county with six fully-equipped and professionally staffed Trauma Centers. These facilities are 100% functional around the clock, every day. The list of participating hospitals is impressive: Children's Hospital and Health Center, Mercy Hospital and Medical Center, Palomar Medical Center, Scripps Memorial Hospital, Sharp Memorial Hospital and UCSD Medical Center. Each of these fine institutions is committed to making trauma care a priority and as a result of their dedication, San Diegan's are blessed with one of the finest life-saving networks anywhere. The U.S. Department of Transportation called San Diego's Trauma System a "model system for the nation."

This showcase system, established in 1984 through the support and leadership of the County and the medical community, offers one of the most notable record of lives saved anywhere. In fact, a person who has sustained a life-threatening injury in San Diego County stands twice as good a chance of surviving than if the injury occurred in nearly any other part of the U.S. As the leading killer of Americans under 44, Trauma is a threat from which no one is immune and a public health problem whose toll is unacceptable and must be addressed. Since it's inception in 1984, the San Diego County Trauma System has reduced the preventable death rate in our county from 33% to less than 2%.

The credit for this remarkable record must be shared with a myriad of life support agencies. Pre-hospital providers which support the Trauma Hospitals include: Life Flight San Diego, Police, Sheriff and Fire departments, Paramedics, Emergency Medical Technicians, dispatch centers and base station hospitals, which provide coordination and communication with pre-hospital transport providers. These pre-hospital providers, along with highly skilled medical professionals and technicians, work together as life-saving Trauma Teams.

Trauma Teams are intimately aware of the crucial element of time in trauma care. Patients who receive proper medical care within the 60 minute "Golden Hour" triple their chances of survival and dramatically reduce the severity of sustained injury. Trauma care is truly a ***"Race For Life."*** ■

The Trauma Research and Education Foundation was incorporated in 1983 as a non-profit organization to represent San Diego's Trauma Care System and enable trauma care providers a means of working together to provide the best possible life-saving system. TREF is dedicated to reducing the number of trauma-related deaths in San Diego by providing educational programs to the public about trauma and trauma prevention. TREF also provides scientific research grants and professional training for trauma care providers.

TRAUMA RESEARCH & EDUCATION FOUNDATION

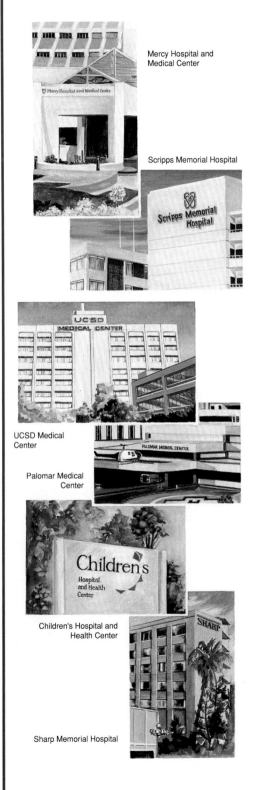

Mercy Hospital and Medical Center

Scripps Memorial Hospital

UCSD Medical Center

Palomar Medical Center

Children's Hospital and Health Center

Sharp Memorial Hospital

Sea World's Commitment to the Sea

Many sailing enthusiasts have experienced the pleasure and delight of seeing a variety of ocean creatures: dolphins bow-riding alongside a swift-moving vessel, pelicans gliding overhead then suddenly turning and diving into the water, sea lions playfully chasing each other in the surf. These are all part of what the ocean offers. Sea World shares the sailor's love for the ocean.

But as those who spend time on the open sea know, the ocean can also be a harsh and uncharitable environment. Storms on the open sea can be devastating to ships; storms also are treacherous for marine inhabitants. Storms give rise to rough and murky waters causing animals to become separated from family groupings, or to succumb to exhaustion due to the physical challenge of turbulent seas. Other environmental challenges exist: ample food sources are not readily available, disease quickly spreads through colonies or herds. Many of these conditions weaken marine animals to the point where they are forced, as a last resort, to find some kind of refuge on land.

Sea World's beached animal program was developed to assist marine mammals that, for whatever reasons, are physically distressed enough to beach themselves. Instituted in 1964, Sea World's inaugural year, the program rescues and rehabilitates between 50 and 475 beached animals (this includes walrus pups, dolphins, pelicans and otters) each year.

Once Sea World is notified of a possible beached animal (most commonly, seals and sea lions), animal care specialists are dispatched to the site to assess the animal's condition. Sea World has been granted a letter of authorization by the National Marine Fisheries Service (a division of the United States Department of Commerce) to recover and rehabilitate beached animals. If the animal is determined to be in need of treatment, it is trans-

Please note that although the animals depicted in the photos are all elephant seal pups, they are not all the same pup in each photo.

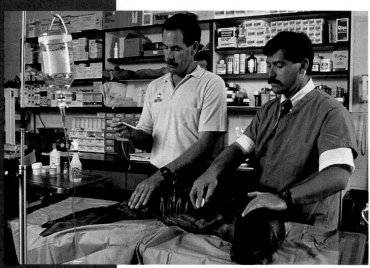

If a beached animal is ever encountered, a lifeguard or a local animal control center should be contacted. They will contact proper facilities. If the beached animal is found in San Diego County, Sea World can be called directly. It should always be remembered that these are wild animals that will defend themselves; they should never be approached except by trained rescue personnel.

ported to Sea World's animal care complex. The behind-the-scenes facility includes a state-of-the-art veterinary laboratory, which houses a surgical suite, automated blood chemistry equipment, microbiology room and a fully stocked pharmacy.

Upon diagnosis by staff veterinarians, treatment is prescribed. Regimens may vary from administration of medication, to surgery, to just plain rest and relaxation. If the animal responds well to treatment, gains weight and strength, and is thought able to compete with animals in the wild, Sea World will release the animal back to the ocean. Sometimes animals suffer chronic complications or physical disabilities which prohibit them from successfully competing with others.

In these cases, animals have remained at Sea World for long-term treatment or have been given a home at another qualified zoological park or aquarium with the appropriate government permits.

In the last 27 years, Sea World has continually expanded its commitment to marine life research, conservation and education. The beached animal program is one way Sea World gives those from the ocean a helping hand.

Scripps Memorial Hospitals

To celebrate the opening of the 1915 Exposition in Balboa Park, one of the promoters asked Alonzo de Jessop if he could assemble 50 of San Diego's private sailboats in the Bay. Confidently, Jessop said yes. He *did* assemble every boat, all 24 of them! In their midst was E.W. Scripp's cutter *Nacky*. This early San Diego sailing memory is one of many shared by the Scripps and Jessop families.

The families are joined, by more than just a love of sailing. Since the founding of Scripps Memorial Hospitals by Miss Ellen Browning Scripps in 1924, members of the two families have provided valued leadership to the Hospitals and their Centers of Excellence. With their help and guidance, Scripps Memorial Hospital, which began as a 44 bed hospital on Prospect Street in La Jolla, is today part of a major county-wide system of healthcare services, and one of the Scripps Institutions of Medicine and Science. It includes three acute care hospitals (in La Jolla, Chula Vista and Encinitas), two convalescent hospitals, and a variety of Centers of Excellence. There are over 1500 physicians on staff, in every specialty. The system serves over 200,000 patients a year, with a commitment to the finest quality health care, respect for the individual, and an efficient use of all our considerable resources.

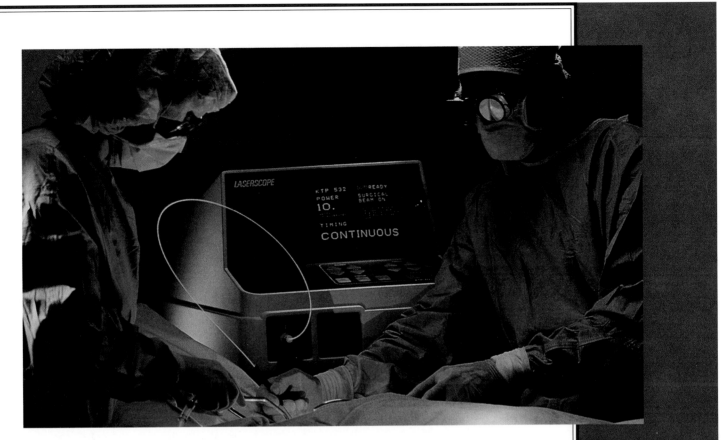

In healthcare, as in sailing, much has changed. Technology now makes possible procedures undreamed of generations ago. One example is the KTP-YAG 532 laser surgical system which allows gall bladder removal through tiny 1/8" incisions. What was once major abdominal surgery, with a minimum three-week recovery and a large, unsightly scar is now virtually a one-day procedure, which leaves almost no trace. Another example, small brain tumors, previously untreatable, are now the focus of extraordinarily precise radiation through a technique called stereotactic radiosurgery.

While the advances in both medicine and sailing would astound our ancestors, they would nevertheless recognize two traits they still have in common: their ability to test the bounds of human achievement and to bring out the best in each of us.

(Above) With The Braemar Challenge Trophy (donated by F.T. Scripps in 1926 to the Mission Bay Yacht Club), and The Jessop Trophy of the San Diego Yacht Club are (left to right): Paul K. Scripps, Chairman of the Board and Editorial Director of John P. Scripps, Newspapers; F. Seth Brown, Vice Chairman, Scripps Bank, member Scripps Memorial Hospitals Foundation Council of Governors, and member Executive Cabinet for the Fund for Greatness; Joseph E. Jessop, Jr., member Scripps Memorial Hospitals Foundation Council of Governors and Chairman of Mericos Eye Institute Board of Governors; and Joseph E. Jessop, Sr., member Scripps Memorial Hospitals Foundation Council of Governors, and Honorary Trustee of The Whittier Institute for Diabetes and Endocrinology Board of Trustees.

Scripps Memorial Hospitals

One of the Scripps Institutions of Medicine and Science

(Left top)
Scripps Memorial Hospital – La Jolla, 1991, part of the Scripps Memorial Hospitals System.

(Left center)
The first Scripps Memorial Hospital, Prospect Street, La Jolla. (Circa 1930.)

(Left bottom)
Miss Ellen Browing Scripps, 1836-1932, Founder of the Scripps Institutions of Medicine and Science

(Right top)
The KTP-YAG 532 laser surgical system is an outstanding example of electro-cardiography, and the use of high tech computers in medicine.

Thanks...

Special thanks to the following contributing
patrons whose support helped realize
Sailing in San Diego – A Pictorial History
(in order of appearance):

—

The San Diego Yacht Club

SAIC - Science Applications International
Corporation

ITT Sheraton Harbor Island San Diego

Dick Stratton & Associates

The Alvarado Hospital Medical Center Campus

Mercy Healthcare San Diego

Race for Life/TREF -
Trauma Research and Education Foundation

Sea World of California

Scripps Memorial Hospitals

—

A portion of the proceeds from *Sailing in San Diego* will go to
benefit the Trauma Research and Education Foundation.